HEADLINES & VOICES

VIRUS
1918

SPANISH INFLUENZA
the words of people who lived it.

Robert John Hadfield

D1607415

A **Thick and Mystic Media, LLC** Production

Cover Design - Thick and Mystic Media, LLC

Editors:
Robert and Judy Hadfield

Special thanks to:
Andrew Hadfield
Steve Walters
Judy Hadfield
Robert Hadfield

Thank you to numerous members of the Audiomover staff for ongoing support and assistance in the studio: Christa, Steve, Tanner, Chris, Andrew, Dylan, Viktor, Lourdes, Sierra and Larae.

Audiobook also available.

audiomover.com

thickandmystic.com

robertjohnhadfield.com

Extra special thanks to Rebecca for keeping me focused beyond who and where I am.

thickandmystic

ISBN: 9798632282093

"After the first little flutter of fear they forget prudence and walk calmly into needless dangers."

The Daily Star - Mirror, Moscow, Idaho, December 10, 1918

Introduction

As the owner of a company like Audiomover, I can't help but be interested in recent history. For nearly twenty years I have worked with people and organizations across the United States archiving obsolete media from the last century; primarily audio tapes, many with significant historical value.

One of the most fascinating, yet overlooked stories in recent history is that of the Spanish Influenza.

To most people it is a story about a virulent disease. A story of a pandemic that ravaged many parts of the world. A story of suffering, fear and death.

No one can be certain of the death toll worldwide, but it is estimated that the Spanish Influenza claimed between 50 million and 100 million victims.

It was so devastating that 1918 was one of those rare periods when the population of the United States actually decreased in size. The population was just over 100 million at the time, and 675,000 people lost their lives as a result of the pandemic. The death rate of those who contracted the disease was as high as 20% in some groups. The scourge didn't seem to have a target either; it killed the young and the old with ferocity. It was alarming that healthy people from 25-35 were particularly hard hit.

And although these statistics tell some of the story, in my opinion, they miss the main part of the story.

To me, the story of the Spanish Influenza is a story about hope and heroism. It is a story about average people rising to the call of their generation.

During the outbreak, the fabric of the United States could have easily come apart, but it miraculously held together. The Espionage and Sedition Acts were passed in 1917 and 1918 respectively and were a direct assault on free speech and liberty. As the Spanish Influenza was ravaging parts of the military, it was kept quiet and downplayed by a willing and/or fearful press. Against the recommendation of medical professionals, the government encouraged giant gatherings related to fundraising for the war - gatherings

2 • VIRUS 1918

which appear to have dramatically increased the spread of the virus. Entire towns were quarantined, whole families died, at least one town as far away from the mainland as Alaska was all but erased from existence.

Governments from the local to the federal level were taking away freedoms, and a vulnerable citizenry was looking for protection and security. That combination generally doesn't end well for the maintenance of liberty.

But rather than accept oppression from both the government and the disease, the yearn for freedom and a desire to control their destiny lifted people above the muzzled media and the fear of death. Of course there were many who ran away from the threat, but there were also many who ran into the danger. Heroes were shaped from the clay of average individuals. People knowingly and actively risked their lives in the war against the disease. Many people died in the fight. Citizens openly questioned the constitutionality of what governments on all levels were asking them to do. Oppressive rules were struck down because people refused to follow them. And at least the Sedition Act was eventually repealed.

In a way, Patrick Henry's declaration, "Give me liberty or give me death," was resurrected in the United States for a moment. People wouldn't stay oppressed or hide in fear. And the scourge that could have permanently altered the idea of liberty in the United States ended up being referred to as the "forgotten disease."

It is partly forgotten because the media of the time largely bowed to the government and didn't cover it thoroughly, but it is also forgotten because the people left it behind and got back to normal quickly.

In a strange act of serendipity, I started a web show in the Audiomover studio where we discuss early twentieth century murder stories recorded in local newspapers. As I searched these century-old papers looking for stories, I regularly stumbled across articles about the Spanish Influenza.

I had heard of the Spanish Influenza, but not much else. So I began reading.

It was early 2020 when I first heard of COVID-19. Having been to China and other Asian countries in recent years, I became more interested in the topic. And as countries around the world became more alarmed with reports of wide-spread death, those Spanish Influenza articles I had been reading took on new meaning.

I remember the H1N1, SARS, MERS, and Avian scares from recent years. And although none of them amounted to anything of epic proportions, they were all an ominous reminder of our vulnerability.

The world has had many pandemics, but none of them were chronicled quite like the Spanish Influenza in the early twentieth century. And even though it was greatly downplayed, much of that day-by-day history can still be found in the country's newspapers. So I have gathered many articles that I think you will find particularly fascinating and created this collection.

Rather than give you broad strokes and rephrase information from the articles, I am going to get out of the way and let them tell their own story. The mission of this book is to let you hear the voices of people in America who experienced the last major pandemic. I have included some brief commentary and contextual information in each chapter to help bring the articles to life.

For some people this book will be absolutely frightening. It is, of course, a record of suffering and tragedy. But I believe you will find the sense of hope and triumph I found in these stories.

Please note: My team has recreated these newspaper articles word for word. We have not edited the grammar, word choice or sentence structure. We have worked tirelessly to re-create accurately the original meaning and content, but still, there are some phrases here and there that are awkward or simply make no sense.

In the early twentieth century, type was placed by hand and newspapers were printed every day so editorial standards were much lower. For example, a person's name might be spelled differently in the same article. In some cases, we have corrected minor spelling errors for the printed and e-versions of the book. In one article we added paragraph breaks to make it easier to read. A couple of times we had to do a little guesswork where it was impossible to read a particular word, but it was never anything that fundamentally altered the meaning of a paragraph.

FINALLY...

This book is organized by topics that flow together smoothly so it can be read easily from cover to cover. For those of you who prefer to focus on specific topics, you can skip around the book without missing critical information.

In either case, I think you will find the information enlightening, fascinating and helpful during this critical part of our country's history.

Chapter 1
A SURVIVOR'S VOICE

"A hearse passed through the boro below here today with three caskets in it, roped on so they wouldn't drop out."

The Lakeland Evening Telegram, Lakeland, Florida, October 17, 1918

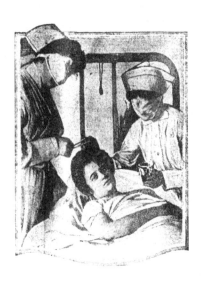

W hen I found this article, I knew I had to share it. It is incredibly well written and captures the daunting sense of despair that was resting like a fog across the country during the Spanish Influenza pandemic.

This is a personal letter from a man named Ben Driscoll, living in Pennsylvania, to family members in Florida. It was printed on page 5 of the Lakeland evening telegram on October 17, 1918. When he wrote the letter in mid-October, the country was in the worst phase of the pandemic. He writes from the perspective of having recently recovered from the Spanish Influenza.

In this letter he references "crepe" on the doors. Crepe is lightweight fabric. When placed on the door of the house, it indicated that someone had died.

The Lakeland Evening Telegram, Lakeland, Florida
October 17, 1918

Ben Driscoll writes from Sharon Hill, Pa., Of influenza scourge.

Mr. And Mrs. M. F. Hetherington, Lakeland, Fla.

Dear Folks: I am lots better tonight, and while I can't say when I will go to work, I hope to at least stay well. I may as the doctor states have to go to the mountains for the cough which this disease left me is weakening me down and I am far from strong. But I will keep you advised of my location as I can't thank you enough for your encouraging letter, which came while I was very sick.

I don't believe that the time God smote the firstborn in Egypt in the days of Herod that grief ever mounted higher to the heavens on hearts braced for shock for the Death of Angels sword, and it does in this section of the state. I know writing does not convey the seriousness or deep feeling of disaster that creep around each home tonight. 3,253 deaths last week in Philadelphia alone. Men and women high up in life dying - priest, sisters, nurses, doctors, manager of big war Industries, policemen, laborers, mothers, children; in fact, it is a plague and one that the U.S. has never had in its history. And still not checked.

Bodies that will be weeks before burial can be had. Sacrifices of doctor and nurses, priests and ministers to assist the sick and afflicted have only ended in death. No church services anywhere. Catholic sisters go to other than their own hospitals to assist the nurses and help pneumonia cases. Coffins, if you want to call them that are piled up in cemeteries. No grave diggers. Funerals must be very short, and none but relatives allowed to attend. Crepe hangs 2 or 3 to a door in many places and for many blocks in town, crepe is all you see on both sides of the street.

One of the Catholic cemeteries has a ditch digger digging trenches to bury the dead till this epidemic is over. Then place them in the family lot. A friend of mine in town lost his wife and the undertaker can't give him any idea when she can be buried. A home near here in which a widowed mother had just received word last week that her son was killed in France, had her only other son, a fine young man and married, stricken last Monday and buried today. His wife is sick with it yet, and his sister went to bed sick today. The priest of the Catholic Church a fine chap is down with it. And his sister in town, who has 6 children, are all down with it, and serious too. Only one minister up and doing what he can to this boro. The rest are all sick.

One doctor came in for lunch yesterday. I think it was 115 calls he had to make. A hearse passed through the boro below here today with three caskets in it, roped on so they wouldn't drop out. It is said that the other day an undertaker had stopped at a house to get a body ready for burial and left the casket on the porch. While inside, working on the body, a man came along in a wagon and stole the casket and took it home and put his own wife in it. She having died four days before. He then buried her. Of course, they won't arrest him, but it only goes to show how desperate they are to have caskets.

It is now about agreed to rent a building and pile the bodies in there until they can be buried when they get caskets enough. If reports received from various places shows conditions just the same, I am sending you a paper in which you can get a glimpse of what we are up against here, and it is bringing serious thought to the minds of us all as to when it will end. Dr. Cornish who is treating me says I had a close call from pneumonia. And while I may have to go to the upper mountains for relief from this cough, even then I am blessed. Of course if I stay here, he doubts as to what will happen as my bronchial tubes are affected and I won't be able to stand anything right now. But then I'm not complaining. One thousand nurses and kitchen helpers are asked for, and many a rich girl is responding even though it means death. Talk about sacrifice! Here is where it shines out in all its full splendor and I don't doubt that the gates of heaven stand wide open to receive those noble souls.

Dreary will be the Sabbath that dawns tomorrow. And as one lady says whose son just died this week from the disease and the other in France, "Well, I'm not visited any heavier than many others." A call was sent out in one boro today for someone to cook and help in a family where the mother and three children were down with the disease, as the father is doing what he can but they need his support and he must return to work. I don't know who they got. But it is a sad case. Many, many little children are now without parents and homes since the past week and they can't put them in the public orphan homes as they may have influenza, too. They have to hold them in hospitals or wherever they can get a place for them until there is no more danger.

> *It is now about agreed to rent a building and pile the bodies in there...*

I hate to say it, but some undertakers have been profiteering. If you offer them $150 to get your loved one burled, some will say, "Nothing doing!" Then if you look prosperous they would say, "Well, give me $500 and I will give you a prompt burial." Isn't it something worthy to lynch men over, which should be done, but it is all in life and anyway, when one gets in this kind of a plague, believe me, it has made an impression on me.

The best people now look at this matter in this light and if you have the disease and you don't get pneumonia, then it is because God is not ready for us.

Life has a deeper meaning now than ever and I can not but feel touched when I come in contact with these facts of sorrow and death.

My cough is worrying me, so I will close for this time.

I do hope and pray that our little city of Lakeland will be spared this monster and I know the hearts of you folks goes out to this section tonight.

Well, goodnight. Best wishes. If I get down again, it may be my last, so I am doing just what the doctor tells me to do and then if I go, well, it is because the Master wants me. But I think the danger is past, if I get in the high mountain country.

As one of the family.

Benj. Driscoll

Chapter 2
THE WARNING

"English physicians are warning their brothers in the United States to be on the lookout for a real epidemic."

Perth Amboy Evening News, Perth Amboy, New Jersey, July 6, 1918

The story of the Spanish Influenza and the story of World War I are inseparably connected. They both impacted each other in tragic ways. Even with the vile and horrifying nature of "the war to end all wars," ten times more Americans died from the Spanish Influenza than were killed in combat during the war. Shockingly, the total number of U.S. citizens killed by the Spanish Influenza was higher than the number of American soldiers killed in combat during all the wars of the twentieth century combined. There were approximately 675,000 people killed in the United States from the Spanish Influenza, and 50-100 million killed across the globe. America was one of the last places to feel its deadly power. As you will see in one of the articles in this chapter, some medical professionals believed the virus wouldn't find our shores.

There is no doubt that the massive movement of troops had a significant effect on the Spanish Influenza's spread through North America, both in its coming from Europe to its dark march across the countryside.

The newspapers kept the American people aware of the activities in Europe – at least what they felt they could. Patriotism was all important in 1918, so anything that presented a negative light on the federal government was avoided. Liberty Loan drives were advertised in newspapers across the country; these were essentially bonds sold to fund the war. The continuous hopeful news about the war was necessary to keep the funds coming, so it was everywhere.

But the messages were clearly missing something.

As I researched old newspapers, I expected to find story after story of death and personal hardship resulting from the Spanish Influenza. But those stories weren't nearly as prolific as I anticipated. With the death of 675,000 people, you would expect it to drown out all other stories.

But there was a reason for the relative silence.

The Espionage Act with its accompanying Sedition Act were passed in 1917 and 1918 respectively. Those acts put a damper on the flow of bad news related to the war or anything that could be seen as speaking negatively against the federal government. It put a fearful cloud over free speech in general. Numerous people were prosecuted under these laws for speaking out against the war.

With that in mind, it's easy to see why newspaper executives might have been reluctant to print bad news related to the Spanish Influenza. Facts about outbreaks in military camps was one of the first casualties of those laws. Unfortunately, certain people in high level positions were afraid the truth might hurt the war effort, send a bad message, demoralize the country, and embolden the Germans. Since the federal government was actively trying to raise money, the fear related to a pandemic would be detrimental to fund raising and to the war effort itself. So many reporters and newspaper executives walked cautiously.

We can be certain that the Spanish Influenza slowed the war to some degree. The Germans may have put off a number of their offenses because of having to deal with the Influenza outbreak among their troops and throughout their own country.

The rapid spread of the Spanish Influenza among the German troops, then to France and England was a harbinger of things to come in America.

The first few articles in this chapter are from July 1918. They are a mixed bag of warnings and assurances. Keep in mind that by September 1918, just two months later, thousands of people along the East Coast were infected. By October 1918, the Spanish Influenza had moved across the heartland of the United States. By November, the countryside had been ravaged with fear and death. By December, it had dramatically slowed down and during January there were comparatively few cases reported. As you read the articles throughout this book, you will see how the citizens of the country went from thinking the flu might not come to America, to being ravaged by fear and death, to being out of the woods in only six months. Although there were three reported outbreaks of the Spanish Influenza, the fall of 1918 is when the majority of the carnage related to the disease took place.

In this chapter, I also included an article from September 1918 that shows the first stages of the American people recognizing there was a problem.

Hindsight a hundred years later makes these articles fascinating. As you consider our own recent epidemics like SARS, MERS and COVID-19, you will see that these articles are frighteningly familiar and ominous.

It is estimated that 228,000 people died from the Spanish Influenza in Britain. It moved through Britain only months before it began its path of terror across the United States. It is believed that the flu was spread by English troops coming home by way of railroad, leaving the disease with unsuspecting people at each stop along the way.

The Sun, New York, New York
July 1, 1918

Influenza epidemic attacks England

London, June 30: Spanish influenza is waging war with praiseworthy neutrality attacking England and Germany with equal severity. In Germany thousands of people are confined to their beds and the army is rife with the malady and it is reported to be spreading in many parts of the country.

In London many business houses are depleted and are spraying their places with disinfectants and providing their employees with quinine. Some offices have provided boxes of quinine capsules, which employees take twice daily as a part of the office routine. At one theater, all the chorus girls have been affected. Telephone systems also are depleted, operators being overcome by the epidemic.

Grimsby fishermen also have suffered. Last week several fishing boats return to port because the crews were overcome with influenza. In another instance more than half the crew of a trawler were taken ill and it was impossible to continue the voyage.

On July 6, 1918, the following warning of a pandemic was in a New Jersey newspaper. You can see the obvious concern that something big was about to happen in America.

In this article you will see the term "La Grippe" used quite often. "La Grippe," "the Grip," or simply, "grip" were used frequently in early twentieth century publications to describe "the flu."

The final line in this article is an example of the types of awkward sentences due to the lower editing standards at the time. Clearly a word was left out during editing or typesetting, but the meaning is still understandable.

**Perth Amboy Evening News, Perth Amboy, New Jersey
July 6, 1918**

Influenza epidemic threatens to spread over whole world

London, July 6: Is the world face to face with another international epidemic of influenza, commonly known in America as "the grippe?"

The obnoxious disease first became epidemic in Spain a few months ago. Even King Alfonso fell a victim to it. Hardly a city or town in Spain escaped.

Then it spread to Germany, and the German army became infected. So widespread was the epidemic in Hunland that the delay in resuming the German drive on the western front has been ascribed to it.

Now the Influenza has spread to England, and whole countries are suffering from it. The epidemic has reached the midlands, schools have been closed to prevent its further spread and many mines and factories are in danger of shutting down.

It seems likely that the epidemic will soon assume the proportions of a pandemic, as in Spain and Germany.

Will the disease spread to the United States and cripple that country's industries also?

The present prevalence of the disease is the most widespread since the world-wide epidemic of 1889, when every country on the globe was affected. There were recurring epidemics in 1893, 1894 and 1895, but they were viewed as recrudescences of the persisting epidemic of several years before.

The grippe plague seems to have no system in spreading itself. It jumps from one country to another, over seas and mountains. That was the case in 1889. In the present epidemic it has jumped France and the English channel to England.

> *It jumps from one country to another, over seas and mountains.*

Of course there is always more or less of la grippe in America, both winter and summer. But English physicians are warning their brothers in the United States to be on the lookout for a real epidemic.

Influenza is extremely Infectious and is caused by a microbe known to scientists as "Pfeiffer's bacillus." The fact that it has a German name is no guarantee that its present spread is due to a German plot to make the whole world sick, for Germany was one of the first nations attacked.

Everybody knows—to his sorrow—the symptoms of the disease, and it is important, if the spread is to be checked, to consult a physician and dose up with quinine immediately they are felt coming on.

During the course of World War I, the United States had some two million soldiers in Europe. The ships with men returning from the war in 1918 dusted the United States with the Spanish Influenza. It would have been impossible to stop it with the untold thousands of soldiers returning home. Over time, these ships became floating hospitals and morgues. Death was so common there was sometimes barely time or energy enough to say a small prayer before sending the body overboard in the middle of the ocean.

You will see in this article that the Spanish Influenza was perceived as a critical problem to overcome, not just to help the masses, but to keep the war effort strong.

The Sun, New York, New York
July 7, 1918

Troop ship turned back by influenza

Health officials fear "Spanish malady" may be brought to United States.
Study of it is urged.
Medical authority says appearance in allied army would be serious.

The fear that the epidemic which has been raging in Spain for more than two months and which has attacked Germany and England may be brought to America has made health officers in Atlantic and Canadian ports watchful.

A troop ship bound for an American Atlantic port was compelled to put into a Canadian port last week because of the prevalence of the disease among the officers and crew, it was learned here yesterday.

The troop ship was two days out of a British port when the men complained of severe headaches, with throat irritation, and then fever. They were unable to work and went to bed, and the day after sweating began, followed by weakness and pains in the muscles and the joints.

On the third day the fever slightly decreased and the dry cough became looser. The general feeling was like that of a case of the grippe.

This is not the first instance of seamen being affected with the Spanish epidemic, for there have been several instances where Grimsby fishermen were compelled to return because the crews were ill with influenza.

Although the epidemic began in Spain early in May, it first appeared on the continent last month. It was presumably carried by German spies traveling from Spain to Germany by submarine and other ways.

The German newspapers have not given much publicity to the spread of the disease in that country, but prisoners taken by the British, French and Americans confirmed tales of the increase of the epidemic in an alarming way, not only among the German people at home but in the German army itself.

Reports have been current for some time along the battle front that the disease was so widespread that it constituted one reason for the German slowness in pushing their offensive aimed at Paris and the channel ports.

An editorial to appear in the forthcoming New York Medical Journal concerning the epidemic in Spain will say:

Attacks Respiratory Tract.

"The fragmentary reports which are to be found in recent British and French medical Journals give evidence of a serious epidemic of an acute catarrhal affection of the respiratory tract which has been raging throughout a large part of Spain since early in May.

"The disease is clearly both epidemic and readily transmitted, if it is correctly reported that in Madrid alone there have been more than 100,000 cases.

> *Relapses are very common and many are attacked twice within a few days.*

"The clinical character of the disease closely resembles that of influenza, but the symptoms seem so far to have been confined to the respiratory tract almost exclusively. The attack develops quite suddenly without premonitory symptoms and is characterized by severe headache tor a few hours, high fever, irritation of the throat, dry cough and slight bronchitis.

There are total loss of appetite, slight gastric disturbance, general weakness and muscular and Joint pains. By the second day there is profuse sweating and the fever decreases, to disappear by the third or fourth day. The cough is somewhat looser and productive after the second day. Relapses are very common and many are attacked twice within a few days.

"The disease seems to affect men especially, women less and scarcely affects children at all. The death rate from it is quite low. No statements are available as to the after effects and the duration of convalescence, but the implication is that recovery is both prompt and complete.

Bacillus Not Yet Isolated.

"Such bacteriological Investigations as have been made have failed to disclose the occurrence of the influenza bacillus, but have shown the frequent presence of an organism resembling the meningococcus. The clinical picture of the disease, its very great epidemicity and the absence of involvement of the nervous system make it very Improbable that the disease is of meningococcal origin. It has been suggested that the organism is the parameningococcus, but even this does not seem plausible.

"A year or more ago we had an epidemic over a large part of this country which resembled grippe quite closely, but which was marked by more severe symptoms than this Spanish outbreak. Very careful bacteriological investigations of the American epidemic showed the absence of the influenza bacillus, but seemed to indicate that the condition was due to a mixed Infection of the respiratory tract in which the streptococcus played a very important role.

"Whatever may prove to be the true cause of the Spanish disease, it is evident that more thorough and painstaking bacteriological investigation must be made.

"While awaiting fuller and more accurate reports concerning the epidemic, its military significance deserves mention. The evident rapidity with which the disease spreads, its capacity for attacking very large numbers in a very brief period of time, and its predilection for the male adult would render its appearance among the allied forces a matter of the gravest concern.

"Every effort should be made to learn its mode or modes of transmission in order to establish effective measures for checking Its spread and keeping it confined to the region to which it is yet limited. What little evidence is at hand suggests that it is communicated from man to man, and possibly also through carriers.

"A thorough study of the conditions in Spain should be undertaken without the least delay as a purely military measure as well as for the relief of the victimized country."

This is a fascinating article in its apparent naiveté. But it's more than likely a propaganda piece meant to pacify the American public. It's hard to imagine that the writer actually believed this, knowing what was happening across Europe.

You can see two obvious goals in this article. First, it downplayed the potential risk of the flu. In the middle of the war effort, the government didn't want any news that would concern the public. The idea of a pandemic would be distracting and discouraging, especially since the country had experienced a pandemic less than thirty years earlier. Second, in order to keep sales of war bonds going, the government needed to focus on the strength of the United States and make it look like the Germans were on the run. This article claims that the flu impacted the Germans primarily because they were weak.

Alexandria Gazette. Alexandria, DC
July 16, 1918

No Influenza in U.S.

New York doctors feel certain epidemic which started in Spain will not come here.

New York, July 15: New York is in little danger of an epidemic of the influenza, which started in Spain and spread to the German armies, according to the medical experts of the city. While little is known about the disease, most of the doctors believe that it is only common grip, and that its prevalence in Spain and Germany is due to the poorly nourished condition of the people.

Commissioner Copeland, of the health department, said there is no cause for alarm, and that he has heard of no new cases of influenza or grip.

"I think the epidemic in Spain," he said, "is a mild duplicate of the one we had in this country in 1889 and 1890, when every one was ill from grip, then a new disease.

"There is nothing for us to worry about. If the reports from Germany are true, saying soldiers are dying from the disease, it means that the resistance of the German people is low. Any disease, even so simple a thing as measles, may cause death if people are not strong."

Dr. Daniel D. Hubbard, of the board of health, said he thought the disease nothing new. "I believe it old-fashioned grip," he said, "and I do not believe that New York is in danger. There is little doubt the epidemic is flourishing in the German armies because the men are in poor physical condition."

Dr. John J. Hill, assistant superintendent at Bellevue Hospital, said he had heard of no cases of Spanish influenza in New York. "We have not had any cases," he said. "I think many of the cases of influenza reported are grip. But in the instances where there have been death there may be some new germ, for influenza rarely causes death except in case of complications, or among young children.

...the epidemic is flourishing in the German armies because the men are in poor physical condition.

"So far as the German army is concerned there are so many things which might have caused illness among the troops, as poor sanitary conditions, bad water or food, that I think there is no reason to believe the Spanish influenza alone has caused it. A similar influenza alone has caused it. A similar case occurred in the typhus scare in Serbia. The epidemic stopped when the cities were cleaned up."

The previous articles in this chapter were from July 1918. I included this next article which was written two months later as a sad contrast to the previous article of assurance. In September 1918, the calming words of propaganda were about to turn into cries of pain and death. Knowing what could be coming, the government seemed to throw their hands in the air because the obvious dramatic steps to slow the progress of the disease were "impossible."

New York Tribune, New York, New York
September 12, 1918

Spanish influenza here, officials fear

Washington, September 11: "Spanish influenza," that strange, prostrating malady which recently ravaged the German army and later spread into France and England, with such discomforting effects on the civil population, has been brought to some of the American Atlantic coast cities, officials here fear, but they are awaiting further investigation and developments before forming definite opinions.

In the opinion of officials, the strange infection has been brought over by people returning on American transports. There is little means of combating the disease except by absolute quarantine, and that obviously is impossible at this time, because it would require interruption of intercourse between communities as drastic as was resorted to in the dread days of yellow fever in the South.

Precautionary measures are considered the best weapons to combat the malady, and, as the disease is a new one to American physicians, the government may possibly take the menace in hand by issuing country-wide warnings and general instructions of how to avoid the infection, if possible, and how best to combat it if it be contracted.

Spanish influenza, although short-lived and of practically no permanent serious results, is a most distressing ailment which prostrates the sufferer for a few days, during which he suffers the acme of discomfort.

Chapter 3
TRAGEDY

*"The casket was placed upon the porch
and the heartbroken mother and daughter
stepped out the door and took a last look
at the face of the dead."*

The Wheeling Intelligence, Wheeling, West Virginia, October 22, 1918

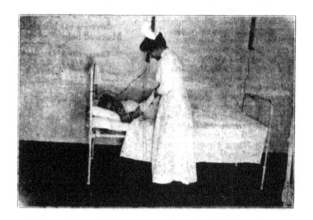

The level of human suffering during the last part of 1918 is difficult to imagine. We are fortunate to have intimate stories describing the pain and anguish of those people preserved in printed publications. There is a great deal we can learn, and strength we can gain, from reading the tragic experiences of those individuals.

Many of the articles in this book were written in October 1918, which was the deadliest month of the plague known as the Spanish Influenza. Almost 200,000 Americans died during that month.

"Spanish Influenza" was of course the common name for the scourge. That being said, it is unlikely this strain of flu had anything to do with Spain.

Spain was neutral during World War I, and while other countries like the United States were squelching potentially demoralizing topics that could impact the war effort, Spain was one of the few countries being truly honest about what was happening with the disease. As a result, the disease became associated with Spain and the connection stuck.

The Bismark Tribune, Bismark, North Dakota
October 24, 1918

Drifts with dead for days in open boat on bosom of Missouri

Mad with delirium.

Aged fishermen discovered on banks of river after lying two days in rain.

After traveling 222 miles in an open boat on the Missouri, with the dead body of his son for company on the last half of the trip and himself delirious with Spanish influenza for a greater part of the journey, with just enough strength left when his boat struck a sandbar opposite old Fort Lincoln to drag himself up on the bank, C. K. Stearns, a 72 year old fisherman was discovered late yesterday afternoon, after lying a day and a night in the rain, and brought to St. Alexius hospital here, where today he shows signs of recovery. The son, who died while the boat was drifting with the current between Washburn and Bismarck, was Thomas Earl Stearns. He had registered for the draft at Plaza.

The mad journey in an open boat was begun two weeks ago. There was very little food. Spanish influenza developed soon after the father and son set out on their voyage, whose destination was Bismarck. For two days both were delirious and then the boy died. That was seven days ago. The father had expected to make the Bismarck boat landing, but he was unconscious when he reached this point, and his boat drifted past, unnoticed in the dusk. Finally the frail craft brought up on a sandbar opposite old Fort Lincoln, south of this city, and after vainly endeavoring to get the boat in shore the father left his boy's body lying in the boat and, taking a thin blanket, waded to shore where he lay down in a sheltered cove to await death. Late Wednesday evening his feeble cries attracted a fisherman, who rushed to Bismarck for help.

For two days both were delirious and then the boy died. That was seven days ago.

Suffers from exposure

When Sheriff French and Coroner Shipp reached the scene in the sheriff's automobile, Stearns was too weak to walk. The constant soaking and exposure had turned his feet and limbs blue, and the feet were so swollen that the shoes could not be removed. He was carried to the car and hurried to Bismarck. At St. Alexius restoratives were administered, and he soon was so far recovered as to be able to give some details of his terrible experience.

Nights of terror and pain

The body of Thomas Earl Stearns the son, was later removed to a local undertaking establishment. His father believes that he died somewhere between Washburn and Bismarck. After the son's death the father was unable to handle the boat, which drifted at will with the current. Rain began to fall Tuesday evening, and all of that night and throughout Wednesday the aged fisherman, ravaged by Spanish influenza, was exposed to a steady downpour. At times he was wild with fever, and weird fantasies thronged round him as his bark drifted on, with the dead body of his son lying inert in the stern. He does not know how long the boat had been stranded on the sandbar when he regained consciousness and after endeavoring without success to dislodge the craft left it there with its somber passenger and made his way to shore.

The Stearns' have for years plied up and down the Missouri river as fishermen. At various times they have fished at the mouth of Apple creek and at other points in the vicinity of Bismarck, where they are well known. More recently they have made their home at Plaza.

Thomas Earl Stearns was 40 years old and was married, but he and his wife had not lived together for some time.

The author of this next article is quick to point out that this sad event took place in Philadelphia, not some small mountain town. Events like this were becoming a common occurrence in big cities as there was a shortage of caskets, hearses and grave diggers. Bodies were piled in alleys or kept in homes for days. There are even stories of young men taking wagons through cities like Philadelphia picking up bodies - similar to what was done during the "plague" epidemic centuries earlier.

Evening Public Ledger, Philadelphia, Pennsylvania
October 12, 1918

Rabbi compelled to cart own son's body to grave

Unable to procure undertaker, I. Rosenfeld, with friend, fashions coffin and conveys grip victim to cemetery where he lowers casket in earth

In a small and unpretentious home at 754 South Third Street sits a sorrowing father who appreciates the gravity of the Influenza epidemic.

He knows to what extent death has gone, and can tell in a sorrowing voice of the aching hearts in South Philadelphia. His own boy, Jack, a senior in the South Philadelphia High School, died a week ago last Friday, and on Tuesday, knowing that the body would decompose unless it was buried, he carried it to the Mt. Carmel Cemetery in Frankford and lowered it into a grave.

...after Jack remained in the house Monday, I decided to bury him myself.

An express wagon was used instead of a hearse and in a rough pine box, fashioned by the father and a friend, the boy was buried. "I was compelled to do it," explained the father today. He is I. Rosenfeld rabbi of the Rumanian Congregation synagogue, at 754 South Third street.

Today Rabbi Rosenfeld told the story of his boy's burial, a burial quite common in the mountain regions of Kentucky, but unknown in Philadelphia until the present epidemic struck the city.

"My boy Jack," said Rabbi Rosenfeld "became sick two weeks ago. I got a doctor, and for a few days it looked as though Jack would get better. Then he began to grow worse, and a week ago Friday he passed away, a victim of pneumonia. I tried to get an undertaker, but it was no use. I simply couldn't get anybody, so, after Jack remained in the house Monday, I decided to bury him myself. With the aid of a friend I constructed a casket, and on Tuesday hired a wagon to cart my boy to the cemetery. Out there I managed to hire a man to dig the grave. I helped to lower my precious boy into the hole, and then came home.

"Jack was such a good boy and such smart boy. And what an end."

This article makes reference to Jacales, which are adobe-style huts. Further down the article also includes stories from other places in the country, listing cities and dates. It was common in these newspapers to publish stories that contained references to similar events happening in places far and wide.

El Paso Harold, El Paso, Texas
October 25, 1918

Influenza toll high on island.

Sheriff says conditions heartrending; hospital at Fabens opens.

"A most pitiful and heartrending condition exists on the Island, where influenza is taking tremendous toll among the natives, particularly the children." sheriff Seth B. Orndorff said Friday. The sheriff had just completed all arrangements for the emergency hospital opened at the school house at Fabens for the treatment of patients from the Island.

"There have been 20 deaths to date on the Island," he said, "and the number of sufferers is over 100, or 50 per cent of the population. Thursday there were seven deaths. Eight of the victims so far have been little school children. Sabin Sierra, the leader of the colony, has lost three of his little ones, while many in other families are at the point of death."

Volunteers Gather Patients.

The nursing at the hospital is under the direction of Miss Ellen Kelly, school principal, while Drs. J. A. Pickett and J. L. Pickett, county health officers, are giving the medical attention, while many volunteer workers are about gathering in patients. Twenty five cots have been installed. The entire expense is being borne by the county.

Conditions Most Pitiful.

"Most pitiful conditions are being encountered, I must repeat." said the sheriff. "Many of the families are too poor even for adobe huts and live in crude "jacales!" One of our doctors entered one of these crude dwellings and, seeing eight persons on the mud floor suffering from influenza, and every opening but one closed, ran out quickly and shouted for the opening of the doors before he could enter.

Refuses Hospital Treatment.

"At another place, the mother was dead. The old grandmother had the body of her daughter stretched out on the mud floor and, outside the hut, had several children lying on the ground in terrible condition from influenza. She refused to have them taken to the hospital.

"Facilities for handling dead people are not numerous in that section and the deaths have been so numerous that the only coffin maker in the neighborhood cannot keep up with them."

> *The old grandmother had the body of her daughter stretched out on the mud floor...*

Sheriff Orndorff had one of the ambulances from the county hospital dispatched to Fabens Friday in order to gather in the sufferers. He was also making arrangements for additional nurses.

Rigorous Action at Globe.

Globe, Ariz, Oct. 25. - With a steady increase in deaths here and in Miami, seven miles from here, as a result of the rapid spread of Spanish influenza, health authorities are taking more rigorous action to halt the spread of the disease. In 24 hours, 19 persons died from influenza and pneumonia in the two towns. Of this number, three died here and 16 in Miami. A total of 134 persons have died in the two towns since the beginning of the epidemic.

Ten more Bisbee deaths.

Bisbee, Ariz., Oct. 25.-There have been ten deaths in Bisbee and its suburbs in 24 hours, ending last night, from pneumonia following influenza. In a statement, Dr. C. Hunt county health officer, said that in the last three weeks there have been approximately 2000 cases of influenza treated by Bisbee physicians. The number of new cases reported now is about 200 daily. In the whole of Cochise County there have been 3700 cases to date. The total number of deaths reported up to date has been 21 in the Warren district and 37 for the whole County, including this district. The pneumonia rate and death rate have been unusually light he said.

Must Wear Gauze Masks.

San Francisco, Calif., Oct. 25.- An ordinance compelling the wearing of gauze masks by every person in San Francisco as a means of preventing the spread of influenza epidemic was passed by the board of supervisors at the request of the board of health. Penalties for violation are fines ranging from $5 to $100 or ten days' imprisonment, or both fine and imprisonment.

The story in this next article was especially tragic in that the victim was a child. It goes on to explain that her death was the result of "complications." This makes sense because she had been sick for at least a week. In some cases, people would show their first signs of illness and die before the day had passed.

The Spanish Influenza didn't have a particular target. It attacked the young and old alike. It was particularly alarming that healthy people between the ages of 25-35 seemed just as susceptible as everyone else.

The Lakeland Evening Telegram, Lakeland, Florida
October 16, 1918

Lula Mae Carter dies after week's illness of influenza

The first death in Lakeland from Spanish influenza occurred last night when Lula Mae Carter, the little ten-year old daughter of Mr. and Mrs. H. B. Carter passed away after a week's illness. This death is a particularly sad one, as a little girl's parents are both ill of the malady, being unable even to sit up, though they are now out of danger.

> *The little girl's condition became critical when complications set in, and last night death relieved her sufferings.*

Mrs. Carter was stricken with the influenza about 10 days ago and a week ago today Lula Mae and her father took their beds. The little girl's condition became critical when complications set in, and last night death relieved her sufferings. She was a child of sweet and lovable disposition, the idol of her fond parents' hearts, and in their great grief the family have the deepest sympathy of the entire community.

The funeral services are being conducted this afternoon at the cemetery, Rev. L. D. Lowe officiating. Miss Thelma Carter and brother, Leonard came in last night from Winter Park, where they have been attending Rollins College, but they reached here after their little sister had passed away. The change for the worse came so suddenly that it was impossible for them to reach here earlier. Two trained nurses and a skilled physician did all in their power for the little one, but all to no avail.

The Leader, formerly owned by Mr. Carter, was closed today out of respect to the family.

This article speaks to the broad impact one, seemingly insignificant person's death, can have. In a bygone era, individuals who worked at the telephone exchange communicated with large numbers of people as they patched lines from callers.

The Idaho Springs Siftings- News, Idaho Springs, Colorado
October 25, 1918

Mayme Cunningham claimed by death

Shocked and grieved beyond expression last Sunday morning, October 20, 1918, the community of Georgetown sadly received the news of the death of Miss Mary Catherine Cunningham, daughter of Mr. and Mrs. Thomas W. Cunningham. Miss Mary, or "Mayme" as she was better known, was another victim of the dreaded Spanish influenza with which the whole country has been so terribly afflicted.

With not a thought of self, but grieving over the sorrow which death had brought into so many homes, Miss Cunningham faithfully remained at her post at the telephone exchange extending words of cheer and sympathy, until, completely exhausted, she was forced to surrender to the disease early in the week before her death.

> ...until, completely exhausted, she was forced to surrender to the disease early in the week before her death.

Miss Cunningham was born in Georgetown July 14, 1895, and spent her life there. She graduated from the Georgetown high school with the class of 1915, and has been a trustworthy employee of the telephone company for over three years, besides assisting in the post office for the past two years. Her father, Thomas W. Cunningham, was formerly sheriff, and is now commissioner of Clear Creek county.

By her winsome smile and laughter, she had woven herself into the lives of those who knew her, and her memory will never be obliterated from the hearts of the many who deplore her departure. Her cheery words and happy expressions will be greatly missed by a long list of admiring friends not only at home, but over the county. Remaining to feel the loss most heavily are the father and mother residing in Georgetown, a sister Mrs. Thomas Garrison of Golden, and a brother Thomas, and to these the heartfelt, sincere sympathy of the entire community is extended.

The remains were laid to rest at Mount Olivet Cemetery Denver, Wednesday.

Services were conducted by Rev. Robert Servant of Golden, Rev. J. J. Donnelly of St. Frances de Sales Church of Denver, and the priest of the Georgetown church Rev. Father M. Boyle. Pallbearers were John Bowen, James Lake, George Gallagher, Walter Farragher, Arthur Hunt, and Frank Thompson.

Many old-time friends of Georgetown now living in Denver, and an aunt, Mrs. J. J. Cunningham of Sterling were present at the burial.

This was one of the saddest articles I found. It combines the ugliness of two horrifying ailments: small pox and the Spanish Influenza. In some communities, funeral attendees were limited to immediate family members. In other communities, people were required to hold funerals outside, and the caskets had to remain closed. In this situation, the mother and daughter were too ill to attend a funeral but arranged to see their dead loved one in an unusual way.

The Wheeling Intelligence, Wheeling, West Virginia
October 22, 1918

Mother and her daughter view dead on porch

Both quarantined in Bellaire home with smallpox and casket brought to them.

Deceased daughter victim of Spanish influenza in Illinois - pathetic incident.

Quarantined in the family home at Bellaire with her daughter, both suffering with smallpox and after entreaties that they might look upon the face of her daughter and sister who died in Illinois of Spanish influenza, the casket was placed upon the porch and the heart-broken mother and daughter stepped out the door and took a last look at the face of the dead. With muffled cries, they stepped back into the house, closed the door and there alone they sat with mental anguish and physical suffering, while the body was silently removed from the porch.

...the heart-broken mother and daughter stepped out the door and took a last look at the face of the dead.

The bereaved mother is Mrs. William Anderson, well-known and highly esteemed resident of South Guernsey street, Bellaire, and her daughter. The other daughter Mrs. William Beihl, wife of a well-known businessman of Wausau, Ill., died in the family home there last week of Spanish influenza. The body arrived in

Bellaire yesterday. When the mother learned that the body had come she pleaded for just one last look upon the face of her daughter. Dr. Boon, City Health officer, was consulted and he permitted the undertaker to place the casket on the porch and then withdraw to permit the mother and sister to view the body.

Mrs. Beihl before her marriage was Miss Minnie Anderson, popular young woman of that city. She leaves besides her husband and parents, two sons, William and Herbert Beihl, and three brothers and three sisters.

After the mother and sister had viewed the body, it was removed to the home of Clark Yocam, sexton of Rose Hill cemetery, where private funeral services will be held this afternoon at 2:30 o'clock. Interment will be in that cemetery.

Patriotism abounded during this time in America. The newly passed Espionage and Sedition Acts ensured that a general attitude of dedication to country permeated the land. Young men, like the one in the following article, were enthused to be involved in the war effort in any way possible. Apparently, this young man had a physical issue that prevented him from serving in a typical way. It is simply called an "ailment of the heart." Although he wasn't going to be able to serve like most young men, he still went to a military base for training. Like so many others, he didn't make it out of the base alive. He reported on October 7 and died from pneumonia caused by the Spanish Influenza on October 23.

Keowee Courier, Keowee, South Carolina
November 20, 1918

Private Ryan W. Mason dead.

Passed away in Military Hospital at Oglethorpe, GA.

Westminster, R. F. D., Nov. 19.- The many friends of Private Ryan William Mason were deeply grieved on learning of his death, which occurred on October 23, in the base hospital at Port Oglethorpe, Ga.

He, with several other young men of the county, who were classified for limited service, was called to Camp Greenleaf on October 7th, for training, and there in a very short time, he developed influenza, pneumonia following, and he was transferred to the Fort Oglethorpe hospital, where he soon passed away.

...brought back to Seneca, accompanied by the father of the deceased, who was with his son in his last moments.

The body was prepared for shipment in Chattanooga-honored with the usual military funeral, and was brought back to Seneca, accompanied by the father of the deceased, who was with his son in his last moments. On the following Saturday, after brief funeral services at the home, conducted by Rev. Walker, of Seneca, and Rev. James Mason, the remains were interred in the Cross Roads cemetery at 4 o'clock, beneath a mound of magnificent floral tributes from the many sympathizing friends.

Private Mason, before being called into service, was a prominent farmer of the county. He was 26 years of age, the oldest son of Mr. and Mrs. W. P. Mason, the father serving Oconee in the House of Representatives the past session, and he was well and favorably known.

In early life Mr. Mason united with the Cross Roads Baptist church, and his honest dealings, natural courtesy and sunny disposition won for him many friends. Anxious to respond to his country's call, though disabled from a weakness of the heart, he was happy, on being given limited service in the thought of doing what he could, though debarred by his physical condition from participating in active service. And when the final summons came he answered, "All is well," and gave up his young life as heroically as the soldier on the battle front.

Surviving are his parents, grandparents, one sister, Miss Winnie, and two brothers, Wyatt and St. John, besides numerous other relatives, to whom much sympathy is extended.

This short article is fascinating. A congressman was married at midnight and was dead from Spanish Influenza by the next morning.

El Paso Harold, El Paso, Texas
October 16, 1918

Rep. Meeker Weds at midnight, succumbs to flu Wednesday morning

St. Louis, Missouri, Oct. 16.- Congressman Jacob E. Meeker died here this morning of Spanish influenza, after his marriage at midnight last night to his private secretary.

Congressman Meeker, a Republican had served two terms in the house of representatives from the St. Louis District. He was renominated in the August primaries. His marriage at midnight to Mrs. Alice Redmond, his secretary, followed announcement by his physician that he could not recover. He was divorced from his first wife. He was 40 years of age.

The Mormon church, also known as The Church of Jesus Christ of Latter-Day Saints, holds a semi-annual conference attended by thousands of members. In 1918, that event would have been held in the historic tabernacle on Temple Square in Salt Lake City. The building holds some 3,500 people. The church's fall conference is referenced in this article as the event that may have helped spread the Spanish Influenza throughout the region. Although there is no direct proof of that, it stands to reason that it could have played a role. The following April, the church postponed conference for two months as the Spanish Influenza was moving into a third wave.

**The Ogden Standard, Ogden, Utah
October 15, 1918**

Six Die of influenza in Salt Lake City

Salt Lake, Oct. 15.- "Send us physicians and nurses at once," was the urgent message sent by Dr. T. B. Beatty, state health commissioner, last night to Surgeon General Rupert Blue at Washington. Hundreds of nurses are needed throughout the state according to Dr. Beatty, and many people are suffering on account of the shortage of doctors and nurses.

Robert J. Shields, head of the Red Cross work in Salt Lake tried vainly for twelve hours yesterday to secure a nurse for a family in Magna, every member of which was helpless with Spanish influenza. Urgent appeals were issued by Dr. Beatty and Mr. Shields for workers willing to volunteer as nurses. Mr. Shields stated that many of the nurses in the city had contracted the disease before the proper precautions had been learned and the disease recognized. As a result the shortage of trained help is very acute.

One hundred and sixty-one new cases of Spanish influenza developed in Salt Lake today, according to the city board of health. Entire families were reported to be prostrated by the malady.

Dr Beatty issued an order to all railroads in Utah yesterday prohibiting the sale of tickets to passengers afflicted with influenza or the transportation of such passengers.

Conference was the event which brought hundreds to Salt Lake and spread the disease, he said.

Six deaths were reported in Salt Lake yesterday as a result of Spanish influenza. Melvin P. Smith 2 1/2 years of age, son of T. W. Smith, died in Salt Lake last night of Spanish influenza. F. J. Miller, a resident of Vernal, Utah died at a local hospital. He contracted the disease four days ago. Azello Garcia, a Mexican, died at a local hospital from pneumonia which developed from influenza. A Japanese died at Judge Mercy hospital early yesterday morning. Mrs. L. A. Rushenburge, 402 Colonial apartment, died at a local hospital last night. Charles Herbert Sutton, aged 26 years, 643 East 5th South, son of Henry and Elizabeth Smith, died at 1:20 this (Tuesday,) morning.

...sixty-five towns reported the disease in Utah.

Dr. Beatty stated last night that sixty-five towns reported the disease in Utah. New towns which reported the presence of Spanish influenza yesterday were Cornish, Devil's Slide, Fielding, Glenwood, Helper, Orderville, Silver City, Storrs, Woodside and Wellsville. He said Ogden had reported two deaths, Sanpete County one, Mt. Pleasant one, and Coalville three. The visit of a soldier who was unaware that he had contracted the disease started the epidemic in Coalville, according to Dr. Beatty and now over fifty cases of influenza have been reported.

Dr. Beatty said that five patients had been put off the train in Ogden suffering from influenza and that the number being taken from the through trains at this point was constantly increasing.

The board of county commissioners voted yesterday to turn over to the Red Cross all county charges who are afflicted with influenza, the county to pay for their care. The patients will be sent to Judge Mercy Hospital. The order concerns only indigent patients who are property county charges and is not an endeavor to provide care for all persons in the county who contract the disorder.

Captain J. M. Dolph, special representative of the military relief corps, is organizing emergency influenza hospitals in neighboring towns. These hospitals will work under the direction of the state board of health. Robert Shields yesterday sent letters to all hospitals in the city urging that all operations not immediately necessary be postponed in order that the nurses may be spared to nurse influenza cases.

Christian Brandley, 32 years of age, a native of Provo, died on the train while returning from Virginia. His wife was to meet him in Salt Lake but received word of his death and went to receive the body in

Ogden. Mr. Brandley went to Virginia about 3 weeks ago to work on special inductions from the draft for munition works.

C. J. A. Lindquist, undertaker, took charge of the body at the station and it was sent to Provo at 9:30 o'clock last night.

Other deaths reported.

Kamas, Utah reported a death from influenza in that District. Henefer reported to the state board of health that several cases had developed and that an isolation hospital had been established.

A message from Coalville last night announced the death from influenza in that city of J. Arthur Beard, 32 years of age. Mr. Beard's wife died of the disease last Wednesday, and at the time of her death both, Mr. Beard and their 9-months-old boy were critically ill. The baby is said to be out of danger.

Mr. Beard was the son of Mr. and Mrs. George Beard and for many years had been employed by the Coalville Co-op, of which his father is manager.

George Lord, who died at Fort Logan Colo. of Spanish influenza, is the son of John and Ellen Lord of 161 Saxon Court. He left Salt Lake on October 2nd. His body is expected to arrive sometime today at the Larkin funeral chapel.

One hundred actors and actresses are out of employment in Salt Lake as a result of the closing of the theaters. Some of the higher salaried artists are well supplied with money while others are far from rich. James Conlon, well known actor, wired to Pat Casey head of the Vaudeville Managers' association in New York and Chicago, asking what he would advise the actors and actresses to do. Mr. Casey replied that his advice was for them to stay in whatever town they were at the present time, and await developments. The artists state that it is the uncertainty of when they can resume their tour which worries them the most. Their salaries stopped when the shows closed.

> *One hundred actors and actresses are out of employment in Salt Lake as a result of the closing of the theaters.*

An example of the indiscriminating deadliness of the Spanish Influenza is described in this article in which father, mother and daughter all die in sequence. It is interesting to note how often people's home addresses were given in newspapers in the early twentieth century. This wasn't just for people who had died. Sometimes a person's address was included to validate an article or statement. For example, if someone gave an endorsement of a product, their name and address would be included with their testimonial in the newspaper.

Evening Public Ledger, Philadelphia, Pennsylvania
October 9, 1918

Influenza kills three of family

Frank Connell, wife and daughter are buried in same grave.

Doctor and nurse die.

Give lives in service of patients at St. Joseph's Hospital.

Father, mother, and daughter, victims of Spanish influenza, will be buried in the one grave at Camden today.

A doctor and a nurse at St. Joseph's Hospital have given their lives to minister to the stricken.

Another woman died within twenty-four hours after the husband she had nursed passed away.

Three members of the Connell family, 123 North twenty-third street, Camden, died of pneumonia contracted through influenza. Frank J. Connell died first. The death of the wife, Mrs. Carey H. Connell, followed. Then their daughter, Florence, ten years old, died. Funeral services will be held at 3:30 o'clock this afternoon, with burial in Arlington Cemetery.

...a student nurse at St. Joseph's Hospital, died at the institution yesterday...

Dr. Edwin M. Smith and Miss Rose Cummings, a student nurse

at St. Joseph's Hospital, died at the institution yesterday, martyrs to duty and ministering to influenza patients. Doctor Smith was born in Valdosta, Ga., and was a fourth-year student at the University of Pennsylvania. He gave his services to the poor during the height of the epidemic and two days ago succumbed, dying yesterday morning.

Miss Cummings lived at 3306 Powelton avenue and had been a nurse in training for a year. She had devoted herself assiduously to the task of attending the ill and several days ago was stricken.

Within twenty-four hours of the death of her husband from pneumonia, developed from influenza, Mrs. Sadie Ulmer died in the home of her mother-in-law, Mrs. Alice Ulmer, Monday. John Ulmer, the husband died Sunday. Their home was at 2002 McKean street. Arrangements for the funeral have not been completed.

The first reported case of Spanish Influenza in the city of Morris, Minnesota, was October 11, 1918. By October 18, one week later, the entire town was put on quarantine. But it was too late to stop the tragedy this family experienced that left two orphans behind.

**Morris Tribune, Morris, Minnesota
November 1, 1918**

Four deaths from influenza this week

Three Die in Pillen family

One of the most heart-rending sights seen in Morris for a long time was the small procession which escorted the remains of three of the Pillen family to the cemetery Wednesday afternoon. It seemed all the more sad by the fact that public funerals were prohibited and no one was permitted to attend except the immediate members of the family.

This is one of the saddest cases in the history of Stevens county. The family were stricken with influenza about two weeks ago and both Mr. and Mrs. Pillen and all four children were taken sick and neighbors waited on them as best they could. Mrs. Pillen's sister, Miss Hendrickson, from South Dakota came and her father, Mr. Hendrickson, from Illinois was also here. Everything possible was done for the family, but pneumonia set in and Mr. Pillen died Wednesday of last week and was buried Friday.

The second one of the family to die was Joseph, 6 years old. He passed away Saturday the day after his father's funeral. Christine, three years old died Monday morning at 2 o'clock and Mrs. Pillen died Monday morning at 5 o'clock.

...public funerals were prohibited and no one was permitted to attend except the immediate members of the family.

All that now remain of this once happy family is a three-months old baby and a four-year old boy. The boy was very sick the first of the week and little hopes were held out for his recovery, but he has improved somewhat during the last few days.

Miss Hendrickson was taken with the influenza last week and for a time it was thought she could not live, but she is greatly improved and getting better. She has performed a heroic service to help those in distress and nearly paid with her life. She is entitled to all the praise and glory which will be bestowed on her.

Chapter 4

NEW RULES FOR SOCIETY

"Handshaking, therefore, is not a harmless if an absurd social performance...should be classed as a felony."

The Sun, New York, New York, October 26, 1919

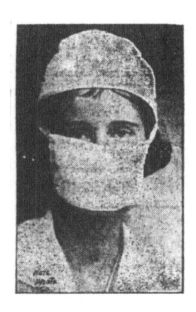

E ven though there was only a rudimentary understanding of viruses in 1918, people were aware that illnesses like the flu were passed from person to person through the air; especially coughs and sneezes. This understanding led to new rules of behavior. One of those rules was the use of gauze masks. These masks covered the mouth, nose and chin. In certain municipalities, wearing them was the law. The law became so strict that some people were even brought to court for not wearing them correctly. This you will see in the following article. The law also created an obvious problem for smokers.

Arizona Republican, Phoenix, Arizona
November 30, 1918

First arrests made for not wearing masks

But fewer actually taken in custody for hearing today, evidently for purpose of testing cases.

In fulfillment of the announcement made yesterday morning that strict enforcement of the order requiring the universal wearing of influenza masks by all persons appearing on the streets would be made that day, the first person to be taken into custody was Edwin C. Moore, an employee of the E. S. Wakelin Grocery Company.

Moore was arrested shortly after noon and taken before Justice De Souza, where he was charged with violation of the health department regulation providing for the compulsory wearing of influenza masks.

He will enter his plea to a misdemeanor charge before Justice De Souza at 2 o'clock this afternoon.

Said he was immune

A few minutes later, V. E. Copeland was arrested for appearing on the street without a mask. He was taken before Justice Wheeler and will be given his preliminary hearing before that Justice at 10 o'clock this morning. He declared he was immune from the flu and would not wear a mask.

A number of young boys were also haled into Justice Wheeler's court, the complaint against them, being that they preferred wearing their masks below the chin. No formal complaint was lodged against them.

But before leaving the court they were fully instructed as to how to wear a mask, the wearing of handkerchiefs in place of gauze being discouraged by the court officers.

No arrests having been made the first day the order became effective, a certain carelessness was manifested in the wearing of masks yesterday.

Must issue warrants

The delay in making arrests was occasioned when it was learned that the police courts would not have jurisdiction in the actions, the health regulations being based on a state statute rather than a city ordinance. Prosecutions for violations of the order will be heard in justice courts, making it necessary for the issuance of warrants and signing of complaints before action can be taken.

...order requiring the universal wearing of influenza masks by all persons appearing on the streets...

George O. Brisbois, chief of police, signed the complaints yesterday making the arrests shortly after L. M. Laney county attorney, handed down an opinion in which he declared the order made by the city health board was valid and that the regulation making the wearing of masks compulsory can be enforced.

The county attorney drew up a special form of complaint to cover the misdemeanor charge, a quantity of the complaints were turned over to the chief of police, under whose direction a vigorous campaign will be waged to stop the spread of the disease by the wearing of masks.

May have invited arrest

It was stated yesterday that several persons were inviting arrest in order to test the validity of the law. It was said that Moore might be among those who are willing to appear as a defendant in an action of this kind, since he was connected with the E. S. Wakelin Grocery company, Mr. Wakelin having been known to oppose the wearing of masks.

The management of the concern with which Moore is connected has devoted space in the newspaper advertising columns in protests against an order which he holds is "dirty, unsanitary, and psychologically in keeping with the ostrich's habit of getting away from danger by hiding its head and leaving its mammoth body exposed. Man is slow to learn that the more of his body he exposes to the air the better."

Police warn many

The first day of the enforcement of the health order making compulsory the wearing of influenza masks found the police in a benevolent mood. For every person who is actually brought into court yesterday for violating the order, four or five technical violators escaped with a warning.

"It's the fellow that struts down the street without a mask to show he won't wear one that we're going to get first," explained Chief of Police Brisbois, explaining that persons who had their masks on, but not in the required position, had simply been warned the first time.

The authorities took the view that when a person had a mask on his chin or dangling from the ear, it showed a willingness to comply, at least in part, with the order. Such persons were merely stopped and told their mask must be over the nose and mouth and kept there.

Stop handkerchief Wearers

Men who cautiously slid their masks down while they inhaled a few "drags" of tobacco smoke were hardly noticed at all by the officers. After all, a man can't smoke with a mask on, and policemen like to smoke as well as anybody.

A number of persons who wore handkerchiefs over the face in lieu of the mask were also stopped by the police and warned. The substitution of handkerchiefs for masks is not well looked upon by health officials, and the practice is being discouraged as much as possible.

Alaska didn't escape the deadly force of the Spanish Influenza. The city of Juneau had its first case on October 14, 1918. Similar to other municipalities, the city council in Juneau created a mask rule and hired additional people to enforce it. They understood the difficulty in enforcing such an ordinance, so they introduced the idea of the "Juneau Spirit" to encourage cooperation.

It appeared at the time that parts of Alaska might get off easy, but a ship from Washington, a place that had been particularly hard hit by the flu, arrived on the Seward Peninsula at the end of the season with the scourge in tow. Apparently, all of the passengers had been checked for symptoms before leaving Washington, but it didn't matter. Alaska natives started getting sick and dying within days. Every person living in the small town of York, Alaska, died of the scourge.

The Alaska Daily Empire, Juneau, Alaska
November 16, 1918,

Get your mask or your money will be needed

NOME, Nov. 15.- Influenza killed 175 natives and 19 whites here. Whole families have died. The epidemic is spreading up and down the coast. Seventy-five soldiers at Fort Davis are ill. It is believed the epidemic is declining among the whites.

Among the white victims were Walter Shields, Martin Anderson, Captain Erickson. There are ten cases at Candle. The epidemic frightens the superstitious natives.

One hundred and fifty cases of Spanish influenza have been reported to Gov. Riggs from Klawack. None of the cases are serious, however, and there have been no deaths.

To Take Supplies.

Gov. Riggs has ordered a fishing boat, the only boat available at Kodiak, to go to Seward to get Dr. Palmer of Anchorage, who will take medical supplies and assistance to fight the Spanish influenza in Kodiak.

More Serum Is Here.

If quarantine regulations are strictly adhered to, the ban on Juneau will be lifted in another week, according to the city health authorities. While new cases were reported this morning, many of those who have been ill with the disease have improved.

Through the efforts of Gov. Thomas Riggs, Jr., 1000 doses of serum vaccine to prevent Spanish influenza were received on the last boat from Seattle. They will be distributed to camps surrounding Juneau to prevent the spread of the disease and to assist in fighting it where it has already spread.

"Gov. Riggs deserves credit for getting the serum here. Only after hammering the Seattle health authorities on the back was he able to secure the 500 doses received first and the 1000 doses just received to be distributed to the camps and towns around Juneau," said Dr. L. O. Sloane, territorial health officer, this morning.

Influenza on Watson.

Several people ill with the Spanish influenza which developed aboard the Admiral Watson on her way from the westward were taken off here this morning and will be cared for in Juneau.

An ordinance providing for the wearing of masks during the present influenza epidemic was passed at the council meeting last night, and upon recommendation of Mayor Emery Valentine a motion prevailed that three special officers be appointed to assist the local police force in enforcing the ordinance.

...providing a fine of $21.00 for those not wearing the masks...

Manager John Spickett of the Palace theatre was present and wanted to know when the theatres would be allowed to open. He said men were allowed to congregate in public places and in card rooms, and he thought this unfair to the theatres. He said their expenses were going ahead without any revenue. The mayor replied under the terms of the ordinance the city health officer was given authority to end the quarantine whenever he deemed it advisable, and the mayor believed that another five days or so, by exercising care, would see the quarantine lifted. The ordinance passed is as follows.

Notice is hereby given that an Ordinance to make the wearing of influenza masks compulsory and providing a fine of $21.00 for those not wearing the masks, was introduced at a Special Meeting of the Common Council Wednesday night, Nov. 13th, 1918, and will again be brought up for final passage Friday night, Nov. 15th, 1918. This ordinance was prepared and introduced at the special request of Dr. L. O. Sloane, City Health Officer and Governor Thomas Riggs, Jr., in order that the epidemic of influenza now raging in our midst may be stamped out without the further loss of life, and the general public is earnestly requested to wear the masks upon our streets and in all public places. This is a duty you owe not only to yourself, but to your fellow citizen, for is not the saving of one human life recompense enough for the few days of discomfort that the wearing of the masks may cause? Show that Juneau spirit, wear your mask for a few days so that we may again open our schools and our commercial activity may become normal once more.

COMMON COUNCIL OF THE CITY OF JUNEAU, ALASKA

I magine living in a city where sneezing without covering could land you in jail. An announcement of New York's new rule was published in this Journal in Iowa.

**Audubon County Journal, Exira, Iowa
October 17, 1918**

Sneezing misdemeanor in New York

New York Oct. 12th- Dr. Herman N. Briggs, state commissioner of health was directed by the public health council of the State Department to take charge of the Spanish Influenza situation in the state. The council adopted a rule making it a misdemeanor for any person to sneeze in a public place anywhere in the state without covering the mouth or nose. Violators will be rigidly prosecuted. Punishment will be $500 fine or one year in prison or both.

Punishment will be $500 fine or one year in prison or both.

Many of the new rules to combat the disease were impossible to enforce. That being the case, it was important to get buy-in from the affected citizenry. To assist in this effort, "clubs" were sometimes organized for the purpose of getting citizens to cooperate; it appears to have worked.

**Evening Public Ledger, Philadelphia, Pennsylvania
October 9, 1918**

Arsenal walkers beat grip

Frankford men go to work on foot, avoiding crowded cars.

Walking clubs are being organized by the employees of Frankford Arsenal as an influenza preventive measure. As the bulk of the arsenal workers crowd the cars and thus expose themselves to the danger of contagion, it was decided that a half-hour walk to and from their homes was better than contracting the disease.

This plan is being urged as probably the only solution to the crowded conditions of the cars, which has been giving officials of the arsenal some concern. Most of the workers live within walking distance of their work, and they are enthusiastic over the scheme to help prevent the spread of influenza and get a little beneficial exercise.

In addition to this, an order has been issued requiring the workers to take exercise in the open air at certain periods. Reports received today indicate that there is some slight decrease in the number of arsenal workers incapacitated by the epidemic

The next two articles are from different papers in Washington D.C., only days apart. It's difficult for us to imagine today, but a wicked spiral of cold and disease was taking place in this community because certain landlords weren't providing sufficient heat to their apartments. Thousands of tenants were adversely impacted because many of them were already sick with the flu. The Commissioner of Washington D.C. set out to fix the problem through legal pressure and shame.

The Washington Times, Washington, DC
October 9, 1918

Landlords are warned by Brownlow to heat apartments they rent

Owners of apartment houses today were requested by Commissioner Brownlow to furnish tenants with sufficient heat as a means of preventing further spread of influenza.

The appeal was put on a patriotic and humanitarian basis, and Commissioner Brownlow said he felt sure his request would meet with hearty co-operation. His statement follows:

"It is extremely dangerous under present conditions not to have heat in apartment houses or homes on these chilly mornings.

"I cannot understand how the most hard-hearted and most shameful profiteers can send his tenant to untimely graves by refusing to furnish heat for the sake of saving a little money off their coal bill.

"I am sure that such a man, if he exists in the District, will be visited with the condemnation of all right-thinking men and women.

"I am advised by the District health officer that on cold mornings and evenings heat is necessary. No action beyond this public notice should be needed for the most parsimonious landlord to start his furnace.

"One case of an apartment house owner refusing to furnish heat, with persons in the apartment ill, has come to my attention. I trust this will be the last and only case so reported. The temperature of living rooms and living apartments should be as near 68 degrees fahrenheit as possible."

The matter was brought to the attention of Commissioner Brownlow in a letter from Capt. Julius I. Peyser, in charge of the Health and Housing Division of the War Department. Several instances of unheated apartments have been reported during the recent cool spell, according to Captain Peyser, and the District Commissioners were asked to issue an order on the subject.

The Washington Herald, Washington, DC October 11, 1918

The failure of certain landlords in the city to respond to the Commissioners' appeal to heat their houses, resulted in a recommendation to the Commissioners yesterday by Dr. Fowler. Dr. Fowler says: "I desire to bring to your attention the serious situation existing in the District of Columbia at the present time by reason of the failure or refusal of the owners of certain apartment houses to furnish heat for their buildings. Seventeen complaints have been received at the Health Department up to noon today relative to the absence of heat in the buildings occupied by the complainants and in each one of these homes, one or more persons are sick.

Thousands of persons are being housed in these buildings and hundreds are sick.

Landlords must give heat

"Thousands of persons are being housed in these buildings and hundreds are sick; to deprive these persons of heat sufficient to remove the chill from their rooms at this season of the year, when the outside temperature is low, will, in my judgment, tend very materially to increase the number of influenza cases now in this District. In many of these buildings patients just recovering from serious illness, with their vitality at a very low ebb, find themselves in an atmosphere which, under normal conditions, to say the least, would be uncomfortable, while in their present weakened condition it is positively dangerous.

"It is not intended, expected, or deemed advisable, or even safe, to have these buildings heated to a high degree of temperature, but sufficient fire should be kept in the furnaces to enable occupants of rooms to maintain a moderate temperature in their rooms, say of approximately 70 degrees.

Better conditions demanded

"With a view to correcting these conditions, it is recommended the Commissioners take such action as may be possible to bring about a betterment of the present conditions."

Reports were made to the Police Department yesterday of twenty-six apartment houses and twelve boarding houses in which no heat is being furnished. In all of these cases persons in the house are reported to be suffering from the disease.

The Commissioners stated last night that Dr. Fowler's recommendation would be given careful and immediate consideration, and if the reports today indicate continued refusal to furnish either enough heat, or any heat at all, immediate action will be taken by the authorities.

If any suffering from the epidemic should die, and it can be proven the landlord had refused to furnish the necessary warmth, prosecution for manslaughter might follow. Capt. Peyser, of the housing committee, believes that many cases of the disease might have been avoided if the heat had been furnished when needed.

This article was written in January 1919, after the worst of the influenza had passed. It must have seemed like a sign that things were getting back to normal. It's important to note that the changes were made because people refused to follow the rules. There comes a time when people want to get back to normal, and not even fear of an unseen disease will stop them.

East Oregonian, Pendleton, Oregon
January 10, 1919

Barbers et al no longer need face ornament

Council by unanimous vote repealed section of Ordnance giving offense.

Had been written in by councilman.

Restaurant men were confronted by trouble from employees.

The provision of Pendleton's new flu ordinance requiring restaurant waiters, barbers, dentists and the workers in a number of other occupations to wear flu masks while engaged in their work was repealed at a special meeting of the city council held last evening. The meeting was called by proclamation of Mayor Vaughan, and the proclamation stated the meeting was called for the purpose of repealing that part of the ordinance providing for the wearing of the masks.

Enforcement of the ordinance threatened to close a number of the restaurants and dining rooms through the refusal of waiters to wear the masks and quitting their jobs rather than to do so. The doctors of the city did not uphold the ordinance, in fact themselves refusing to wear masks, and the restaurant workers and others required to wear them used this as a leverage, taking the ground that it was not a proper requirement. The trouble yesterday, however, was precipitated by the arrest of Louis Pinson, of the Office Lunch, for failure to wear a mask. Since the repeal, this case will be dropped.

Not in original draft.

Discussion before the vote brought out the fact that the "flu mask" provision was not in the original draft of the ordinance as prepared by City Attorney Fee, but was written in it before being passed at the request of councilman at the meeting. Colonel J. H. Raley was present at the meeting last night as a representative of the restaurant men, and in their behalf stated their position in the matter.

Vote was unanimous.

The vote on the repeal was unanimous. Councilman present and voting were: Estes Ell, King, McMonies, Friedly, Folsom, this being the first meeting of the year at which the last named has been present. Absent Penland and Chairman Taylor.

Repealing the flu mask requirement in no way affects the rest of the ordinance.

...people are not allowed to get closer than four feet to each other.

The number of people to be allowed in store rooms is still limited to one to each 100 square feet. Crowds are not allowed to gather at the depots. In transacting business people are not allowed to get closer than four feet to each other. Pool rooms are limited to two players to a table. Churches can be opened provided those attending are limited to one to each 100 square feet.

Special officers for enforcing the ordinance together with the quarantine regulations are continued as before.

This is a broad-reaching article that starts out with an almost comical discussion about handshaking. It was written a year after the worst of the pandemic and the writer shares interesting statistics and lessons learned.

The Sun, New York , New York
October 26, 1919

Influenza warning brands handshaking as deadly

National Health officials in Crusade against possible recurrence of epidemic point out that the germ still lurks in our midst and urge every precaution.

BY JAMES B. MORROW.

There is no way of learning how many persons in the United States are killed each year by the procedure known as handshaking or how many are made ill and take to their beds for long or short periods.

Esthetically, of course, handshaking is ridiculous. Practically it is a waste of time and energy. Hygienically it is little short of being murderous. A clean man goes forth in the morning only to return in the evening reeking with germs of all descriptions, most of which he has acquired from the friends whom he has met in and out of his shop, store or office.

Each friend, so to say, specializes in a particular kind of germ. Or he may be a hive for colonies of various species of organisms. Anyway, the clean man goes home to his wife and children teeming with the invisible agents of death and suffering.

He may have washed his hands twenty times from 9 A. M. to 5 P. M. and still he teams, because in the short intervals between his ablutions he has ruffled his hair, pulled his mustache and stroked his chin, and thus has given general circulation to such germs as may have been localized temporarily on his nails and fingers.

Sanitarians with a gift toward statistics are sure that the average man touches his face and head several hundred times each day with his hands, and hands, as it were, freighted with destruction. The war just ended was a horrible event. About 50,000 young Americans gave up their lives in France.

But last winter 550,000 men, women and children died in this country from influenza. And 25,000,000 other men, women and children had the disease but lived through It.

Handshaking, therefore, is not a harmless if an absurd social performance. It never had any standing in common sense. Possibly it now should be classed as a felony.

Everything Would Be Blue

If the moisture in one's mouth, says Dr. Charles V. Chapin, the famous author and health officer of Providence, were blue and not colorless, one's hands would be blue and one would then realize how often one's fingers found their way to the lips and contiguous surfaces. Always when talking, singing, coughing or sneezing one is spraying the air with a colorless fluid which, if it were blue, as Dr. Chapin points out, would cause alarm as well as disgust.

...the clean man goes home to his wife and children teeming with the invisible agents of death and suffering.

The world then would be blue, surely enough. Picture, for example, a male with a beard dyed by himself and the men and women with whom he daily conversed. Or a beautiful young maiden, speckled like an Easter egg from her forehead down to the point where modistes now draw their retreating boundary.

It is not a specially pleasant task to write about defiled hands and germs diffused into the air through open mouths, but these are physical practices that should be ended and alarm signals that ought to be run up. The influenza has not been "stamped out."

Last winter every one was told over and over again to cough or sneeze into his handkerchief. How many men or women paid any attention whatever to that particular item of counsel? In churches and theatres and on street cars workingman and capitalist, society woman and domestic, coughed straight at one another and openly sneezed altogether until clean and well mannered persons seriously thought of going into their own houses and staying there.

Again the health officers of the nation are sending warnings into every part of the country pertaining to the probable recurrence of the scourge that was so deadly and otherwise so disastrous a year ago. And the writer has volunteered his help in the matter. Again, although much has been printed concerning influenza, there are phases of the subject that are familiar to only a limited number of the laity. Also there is a news side to the present situation.

Worst Ever Known.

A good many persons, possibly, will be surprised to learn that Influenza, normally, causes from 15,000 to 16,000 deaths yearly in the United States. At any rate, such was the fact up to the beginning of the pandemic in August, 1918.

Pandemic, the dictionary defines, means "Incident to a whole people." Influenza was a pandemic disease last year. Only a few isolated or mountainous settlements escaped attack. Dr. Raymond Pearle of Johns Hopkins University and an expert in vital statistics says that "the pandemic of influenza which swept over the world in 1918 was the most severe outbreak of the disease which has ever been known."

And all the while, or for many years, at all events, the Influenza was prevalent, here and there, throughout the United States. Suddenly, so it seems, the virus turned aggressively virulent and spread in all directions. Epidemics of influenza have occurred in this country since 1647, when germs of the disease were brought here from Spain. The epidemic of 1889 and 1890 originated in the Orient, extended into Russia and in time reached the United States.

A study of the disease shows, seemingly, that during the years when it is more or less quiescent it is gaining and conserving its strength for a mighty attack on the human race. The United States Public Health Service, of which Dr. Rupert Blue is Surgeon-General, does not believe that the pandemic last year was caused by fresh germs brought from abroad. It was the old germs, long established in this country and causing many unnoticed deaths each year, that killed 550,000 Americans within a few months and caused 25,000,000 other Americans to become ill.

...to attack mankind on every front and depopulate the world.

It was not until September last year that, "the epidemic first attracted attention in the United States," although an outbreak of Influenza had occurred in Boston on August 28. And yet a mild type of the disease had been prevalent in twenty-two States as early as January, 1916.

In a sense, influenza developed contemporaneously in all parts of the universe-just as if the germs, countless in number and fully equipped with the deadliest of poison, had determined, after a long period of preparation, to attack mankind on every front and depopulate the world.

As early as June, 1918, influenza was reported as being present in such widely separated cities as Zurich, in Switzerland: Birmingham, in England; Bombay, in India, and Santos, in Brazil. By July it was in Holland, Norway, Sweden, China and Algeria. It was now epidemic throughout Switzerland.

In August, as was stated, came the outbreak in Boston. Meanwhile it had appeared in Spain, Greece and the West Indies. During September the disease was reported from Corea, Tunis and South Africa and was epidemic in three cities of Canada. Within a month after its appearance in Boston, the disease was causing many deaths in forty-three States and the District of Columbia. By October it had spread over the entire country, killing its victims everywhere, except in "the more isolated rural and mountain areas."

Russia, Liberia, Australia, Madagascar, Cuba, Porto Rico and Hawaii were attacked in the month of October; Arabia and Samoa in November. Could the germs have been carried by travelers into every part of the world almost simultaneously? Sanitarians by and by will settle that question. On the face of known facts, it would seem that the uprising of the influenza germs was practically simultaneous in Europe, America, Asia and Africa.

Some time, possibly, there will be a Jean Henri Fabre who will attribute to germs the instincts, purposes and philosophies that Fabre himself gave to spiders. But before the Influenza germ can be biographied he must be found. Up to the present, he appears to have escaped the pursuit of man and the identification of microscopes.

Scientists, in their excuse for defeat, explain that some organisms, meaning germs, are so small that no porcelain filter will hold them and so they slip through, along with the liquid containing them, and remain unknown and undescribed.

Baffled by a Germ.

"There is still some uncertainty as to the nature of the micro-organism causing pandemic influenza," confesses the United States Public Health Service. This is a guarded statement, to say the least. The truth is that the germ has not been positively identified.

Referring to his own investigations Dr. Edwin O. Jordan, one of the greatest of bacteriologists, says that "they have not shown the predominance or constant presence of any one organism in the upper respiratory tract of Influenza patients. The Pfeiffer bacillus, however, has been more conspicuous than any other organism." This germ is very small, is rod shaped and was discovered by the man after whom it was named.

It is difficult, if not impossible, to destroy an unseen enemy. There can be no cure for influenza except through accident until the germ causing the disease is captured and some method is found, by experimentation, for its extermination.

Four of the most eminent of germ hunters are now engaged in a campaign against the influenza bacillus. They are William H. Park, professor of bacteriology and hygiene at Bellevue Hospital and Medical College, New York; George W. McCoy, one of the great specialists of the United States Public Health Service and an investigator of the plague and of leprosy; Milton J. Rosenau, professor of preventive medicine and hygiene at the Harvard Medical School, and Edwin O. Jordan, professor of bacteriology at the University of Chicago.

Meanwhile, of course, other sanitarians and bacteriologists are hard at work, and it is altogether likely that the influenza germ soon will be isolated, that is caught, either in this country or in Europe. Until that has been accomplished, as has been pointed out, no cure for the disease can be provided. "So far as the most careful scientific investigations have been able to determine," says the Public Health Service in one of its statements to the American people, "no cure has been discovered. The suggested remedies which give the most encouragement are even now in their experimental stage."

This statement was made as a warning against quack doctors and false medicines. While no cure is yet available, and, consequently, no positive preventive has been found, every one can obtain a large measure of protection by following the simple rules recommended by the national health authorities.

These rules have been printed over and over again in every part of the country. It is stated, for instance, unqualifiedly that "influenza is spread by direct and Indirect contact." Coughing in one's face while hanging on a strap in a street car, or on the back of one's head while at church or the theatre, comes under the heading of direct contact.

Those who with abhorrence have seen drivers of bakery wagons deliver bread at grocery stores, pawing and clutching the loaves with their vile hands, washed perhaps twice a day, recognize one of "the paths of Infection" opened and maintained in prime order by that ever busy old reprobate, Direct Contact.

Some day a nauseated and shuddering cynic will write an article entitled: "Really, is civilized man and the dainty wife of his bosom naturally cleanly?" Vanity and the manicurists have wrought a little improvement in one woefully neglected direction, and the latter, no matter what may be said of a few of them, are deserving of more praise than they will ever receive.

Direct contact cannot be done away with altogether, but it can be reduced. The man at your side, Mr. Reader, or Mrs. Reader, may be a germ carrier parading under the banner of health. There are plenty of such human vehicles of illness and death. Pollution may be in his breath and an unseen coffin on his shoulder. Order him to stand back. If not in words, then in manner or looks.

Pollution may be in his breath and an unseen coffin on his shoulder.

The prepared person, it goes without saying, like a nation that is so wise and so blessed, is ready for the onslaughts of his enemies, whether they be germs or animals belonging to the same species as himself.

Where Man Battles.

His citadel, when germs attack, is his stomach. In that arsenal and fortification he keeps his arms and ammunition. Also his troops. From that centre his host goes forth to battle and to die or conquer.

Diet, then, is secondary to no other measure of defense against Influenza. In it is strength and all necessary regulatory processes, so one of the very able experts in Washington asserts. "Taking medicine for the stomach is overdone in the United States," he said to the writer.

This man, Dr. Joseph W. Schereschewsky, began twenty years ago a scientific study of diseases for the national Government. "Moreover," he added, "we Americans eat entirely too much concentrated food.

Meat, for example. What we need is more roughage-cabbage, beets, carrots, turnips and spinach-and more stewed fruits. Such a diet, with the physical exercise of walking and fresh air day and night, will make the doctoring of the stomach unnecessary in most cases."

The "paths of disease," as the sanitarians say, are many and by this time so distinctly marked that they should be known to everybody. Ordinary germs have two main highways-the human nose and mouth. But the methods they employ, or that are employed, of entering the nose and mouth are almost limitless in number.

Germs get into water and milk, into food, onto towels and napkins, onto knives and forks, into cups and tumblers. Likewise into the air. These elementary facts are well understood, but when such a disease as influenza of the virulent type declares war on the human race it almost seems as if man pulls down his defenses, gets out of his trenches, marches into the open and challenges the germs to come on with their artillery and battalions.

And when the battle begins, man, apparently, has but a single Idea. He watches his food or he watches his drink, or, as with influenza, he cover his nose with a strip of gauze, whereas he should do all three. Germs, like the Huns when they are at war, "filter through" any and all openings.

The Public Health Service believes it to be necessary to keep on repeating its counsels and warnings to the people. "Recurrences," it says to-day and will say to-morrow, "are characteristic of influenza epidemics, and the history of the last pandemic and previous ones would seem to point to the conclusion that this one has not yet run its full course.

"It seems probable," the statement continues, "that we may expect at least local recurrences in the near future, with an increase over the normal mortality from pneumonia for perhaps several years."

Mysteries that Continue.

All physicians realize that the state of mind acts and reacts on the body. Terror weakens nature's defenses. Men and women in some instances take to their beds through the primary cause of fear and worry. The officials in Washington do not desire to alarm the country, but they would fail in their duty were they to say that danger from influenza no longer should be seriously considered. The danger is present. And the mysteries of influenza are as baffling as ever.

Why did the disease attack only 15 per cent of the inhabitants of Louisville and more than 53 per cent of the inhabitants of San Antonio? And why is the case incidence, as it is called, highest in children from 5 to 14 years old? Furthermore, why are more women than men of the same age stricken by the malady?

Differences, if any, of air and environment do not account for a death rate of influenza and all forms of pneumonia of 6.5 per 1,000 population in Buffalo and 4.8 in Rochester; of 5.4 in Cleveland and 3.4 in Toledo; of 7.9 in Boston and 6.4 in Lowell; of 5.6 in Los Angeles and 7.9 in San Francisco; of 8.8 in Philadelphia and 9.6 in Pittsburg.

Stated in a more startling fashion, the deaths for 25 weeks ending March 1 this year were 3,075 in Buffalo and 1,274 in Rochester; 4,405 in Cleveland and 885 in Toledo; 6,183 in Boston and 695 in Lowell; 3,785 in San Francisco and 3,193 in Los Angeles; 12,790 in Philadelphia and 4,743 in Pittsburg.

"There are notably wide differences in the mortality rates of individual cities in the same section, even between cities close together," say the Public Health Service, "differences which are not as yet explained on the basis of climate, density of population, character of preventive measures exercised or any other determined environmental factor."

Rough figures show that from thirty to fifty persons in every 100 are "susceptible" to the germs of influenza. That being so, the disease is actually more of a menace than is realized by laymen, dreadful though the known toll of death was last winter.

Washington is neglecting no precaution that can be taken to meet and modify a recurrence of the epidemic during the approaching months. States and cities are expected to take care of their own people. The commissioner of health in each State, however, has been asked to give the national Government the names of 100 physicians who could and would respond to calls for help from regions requiring immediate medical attention.

In the meantime the four eminent bacteriologists heretofore mentioned and scores of others in this country and Europe, as has been stated, will endeavor to discover the influenza germ and then to find a means of killing him.

Chapter 5
SHORTAGES

"Seven bodies were placed in the morgue at Rock Creek Cemetery today because men could not be secured to dig graves."

The Washington Times, Washington, DC, October 8, 1918

In times of catastrophe, there are always shortages. In times of a pandemic, shortages come in all forms: time, resources, goods, services, people, etc. This is why, when facing something like the COVID-19 pandemic, governments try to "flatten the curve." As a society, we have learned from experience that a medical system can be brought to the edge of collapse if it is overwhelmed by too many people needing medical assistance too quickly.

Such was the case with the Spanish Influenza. Shortages weren't limited to doctors, nurses, hospitals and medical resources. They also included caskets, mortuary space, and gravediggers. Many people had to deal with medical shortages by staying home. Some had to deal with death by taking things into their own hands. Bodies were often kept in houses, piled up in alleys for days, or placed in common or temporary graves. Some people had to resort to building their own caskets or using blankets to bury their dead.

The articles I included in this chapter give great examples of the shortages felt across the country.

The Washington Times, Washington, DC
October 8, 1918

Cemeteries call for gravediggers

Coincident with the rising of the daily death rate from Spanish Influenza, comes the information that grave diggers can only be secured at a premium. Every large cemetery in the District reports a serious shortage. The draft took many of the men. Government jobs have taken others. The influenza has incapacitated more.

At Glenwood Cemetery today with sixteen listed, two of the six gravediggers reported for work.

Seven bodies were placed in the morgue at Rock Creek Cemetery today because men could not be secured to dig graves.

Congressional and Mount Olivet cemeteries reported a situation almost as bad.

Gravediggers are paid $3.50 for an eight-hour day.

This article describes the desperate call for medical helpers in one city. As you read the article, you will see why the call was needed. The death toll and the massive number of people infected with the virus were clearly beginning to overwhelm the system.

It is interesting to note that this request from Salt Lake City was made to Rupert Blue, the Surgeon General of the United States. His name is seen in many of the newspaper articles during this time.

The reason for the shortage of medical staff wasn't just because of the pandemic; it was also a result of the war effort. Many doctors and nurses across the country had been sent to Europe to support the hundreds of thousands of troops. This resulted in many hospitals around the country being understaffed. When the outbreak of Influenza hit stateside, the shorthanded medical community was unable to keep up.

The Ogden Standard, Ogden, Utah
October 25, 1918

Trained nurses are wanted at once in Salt Lake

SALT LAKE, Oct. 25 -Dr. T. B. Beatty wired to Surgeon-General Rupert Blue at Washington, D. C., last night for twelve trained nurses. Dr. Beatty says the nurses are needed at once.

The death toll in Salt Lake yesterday follows: Mrs. J. E. Coon, Thirty-third South street, died while a nurse was on her way to the residence in answer to an emergency call sent to the Red Cross by a neighbor. Mrs. J. C. Yeancy, 22 years of age, a resident of Magna, died at the Red Cross hospital. James A. Sakins, 31 years of age, died at a local hospital. Ada Helming, 45 years of age, died at a local hospital. Woodrow Jorgenson, 1 year old, died at a local hospital. Mrs. Mae B. Wende, 39 years of age, died last night.

Evelyn McCarty, daughter of Mr. and Mrs. Samuel McCarty of 205 Paxton avenue, died at a local hospital yesterday of influenza-pneumonia. The body will be shipped to Ogden for burial.

Licklin Christine Jensen, daughter of Nels P. Jensen, 752 Parker's lane, died yesterday of influenza. She is survived also by two brothers, Charles and Merrill.

The number of Influenza cases reported to the city board of health since the epidemic started is 1700. Dr. Samuel G. Paul, city health commissioner, stated that many doctors of the city were neglecting to report all their cases as they were so busy. He urged that each case be reported as soon as possible.

Officers co-operate

Dean W. W. Fleetwood, who represents the Red Cross under the direction of Dr. Beatty, said that not as many calls for help had been received at Red Cross headquarters as usual and the cases in the city had not proved distressing. Dean Fleetwood visited Ogden Wednesday night and he reports that splendid co-operation exists between the Red Cross and the health authorities in that city.

Yesterday a man reported to the Red Cross headquarters for duty in nursing the sick. He stated that he found he was too old to go to the front but he could cook and was willing to look after needy families. He arranged his business affairs so that he could go on duty this morning as his services were eagerly accepted. The "Silent Moment," or the simple ceremony of the Red Cross workers held at noon each day of pausing during work for one minute and thinking of the boys at the front and wishing them well, went into effect yesterday noon at Red Cross headquarters.

Three members of the same family, all victims of influenza were buried in Lehi yesterday.

Rainer was one of the new towns to report cases of influenza, yesterday. Twenty cases and one death were reported there. Standardville has declared a strict quarantine but no case has yet appeared. Kanosh, Hyrum and Centerville all reported the presence of influenza for the first time yesterday. Park City pool halls were ordered closed today by Dr Beatty. The town has obeyed the quarantine rules with the exception of closing of the pool halls.

The number of new cases of influenza admitted to the post hospital at Fort Douglas yesterday showed a marked decrease. The total new admittances for the day was fifteen cases. Those in the hospital are continuing to improve and patients are being discharged daily as recovered. The quarantine at the post is still being strictly enforced in an effort to get the malady under control and will be enforced until it has disappeared.

Three members of the same family, all victims of influenza were buried in Lehi yesterday. They were Charles Goates, his daughter Vesta, 8 years of age, and Elaine, 6 years of age. Kenneth Goates 10 years of age, was buried Sunday. All four died in Ogden where Mr. Goates was superintendent of the State Industrial farm. Beaver reports the death of Stanley Edwards, 23 years of age and Ambrose Harris, 26 years of age. Lamar Van Wagenen, 25 years of age, died Wednesday at Midway, Wasatch county. Funeral services will be held today at 10 a. m. J. J. Hunt, a prominent stock man of Rexburg, Idaho, died while returning to that city from the east of influenza. Funeral services will be held Sunday in Rexburg.

Morgan, Utah, is reported to be suffering severely with the disease. Eleven deaths have occurred since the epidemic started and there are now 245 cases in the town. Three Salt Lake nurses are coping with the situation.

This article describes the overwhelming nature of the pandemic. As the headline states, medical personnel were unable to answer all the incoming calls. What fascinates me about this article is the call for citizens to provide names and addresses of potential helpers. As the article says, they wanted to find the people who "have refrained from lending any assistance whatever."

The Ogden Standard, Ogden, Utah
November 25, 1918

Twenty calls could not be answered last night

"There was an unusual call upon the local Red Cross yesterday for experienced nurses," says Rev. J. E. Carver. "At least twenty calls were left unanswered because there was no one to send. The condition in Ogden has shifted from a need for volunteer untrained help to a most urgent demand for men and women who have had experience in nursing. This is due to the presence of a large number of serious cases, and also to the fact that so many of the sufferers are in homes where skilled nurses can well be afforded. There will be an attempt tonight to meet the calls for help but there is a work now for every citizen of Ogden in helping in the following manner:

"The Red Cross desires a complete list of the women who have had some experience in nursing. Any person knowing the name and address of any nurses will be doing a real assistance by telephoning their names to the Red Cross. It is hoped in this way to secure several added workers. It is thought that there are many in the city who might be of valued help if their names could be secured and pressure brought upon them to lend their aid in this stress.

"The need still continues for all who will volunteer to help as untrained workers. Some of these have been as effective as the trained assistants. They can work under the direction of the doctor in charge under the supervision of the Red Cross visiting nurse or a trained nurse.

"There have been very few of these volunteers in the past few days and any who have had the influenza can be real helpers in this way without danger. It is hoped that many will realize that one of the best methods of meeting the malady is in taking proper care of those who have it now. The Red Cross can use twenty nurses tonight, if they can be secured.

"There is another need that the Red Cross wishes to help in meeting. There are many homes wherein a maid of all work is badly needed. The mother and father are sick and the meals must be provided and the fires kept up and needed things attended to. Many such helpers are needed at once. If the people of Ogden will make a personal duty to help by telephoning all of these helpers they are sure can be secured, much good will be done. Be sure, however, the persons whose names are telephoned will serve and thus conserve the time of the Red Cross workers for needed things.

"One evident fact should be borne in mind by those who desire help. It is unfair for any who have relatives who should assist in caring for them to ask strangers to come to their homes and do the work their own kin should perform. This, of course, applies only to calls for volunteer aid. There have been calls received for volunteer help, when, upon examination, it was found that those asking wished strangers to do the work that near relatives should perform. Some of the best free workers have been thus imposed upon and the result is discouraging, to say the least. The Red Cross will not send free help to homes unless such help is not possible to secure by any other means, or the inmates of the home have no one to whom they can turn for aid.

> The Red Cross desires a complete list of the women who have had some experience in nursing.

"If the people of the city will assist by sending the address of any helpers to the Red Cross, the Red Cross will place them wherever they are most needed. The Red Cross, however, can only send out the helpers who volunteer or whose location they know. It is the conviction of many that there are several in Ogden whose training and ability is needed right now but they have refrained from lending any assistance whatever.

If you can't nurse or help by going yourself be a true aid by assisting in securing one who can. Send in their names to the Red Cross."

This article describes the feelings of desperation caused by shortages. It also has an important theme: "The flu is a calamity for everyone."

During a pandemic, no one gets away unharmed. Even if you never get ill, the societal and economic effects will find you, and leave you damaged in their wake.

The cry for help in this article is obvious and gets to the heart of the shortages. The writer makes the point that many people who would otherwise survive are dying because they can't receive "ordinary care." This demonstrates the danger that can result from an overwhelmed system. The general lack of medical care hurts everyone needing the assistance of a skilled medical practitioner. Indeed, as the headline states it's "everybody's calamity."

Evening Star, Washington, DC
October 16, 1918

Visitation of influenza is rated everybody's calamity

"The plague came and all men served their stricken brothers, save those who deserve not the name of man."

This epidemic of ours is not to be dismissed as a misfortune which one has happily escaped. It is everybody's calamity, since suffering knows neither sex nor class lines, and there is not a man or woman of us who can afford to ignore it. Neither is it a sensational exaggeration-there are the obituary columns to prove it. There is nothing more convincing than a death notice.

...many men and women-our own men and women-are dying for want of ordinary care.

If anyone doubts the situation, go for information to the public health service, which has its headquarters in the Webster School at 10th and H streets northwest. You will find men and women grimly alert every hour, day and night, to supply whatever aid may be needed-fuel and food, if necessary, and nurses-so long as nurses maybe had.

Lack of nurses overwhelms.

It is the lack of nurses that is the overwhelming want of the situation. Practically every trained and experienced volunteer in the city is working, regardless of personal health, but-nurses are only human. And for that reason many men and women-our own men and women-are dying for want of ordinary care.

Dr. Mustard and his assistants of the public health service are not asking for experienced nurses. They are begging for helpers who possess ability and humanity enough to hand a stricken soul a drink of water, and to do the small vital things that a sick room demands.

If you had gone to the Webster building today they would have told you, for one case, of a family of nine-two dead and seven too ill to help themselves.

And in the telling other cases were reported of like helplessness, which, if we do not remedy with our personal help, then the poet was entirely right about man's inhumanity to man.

Relief stations established.

The public health service has installed relief stations in each of the four sections of the city.

Station No. 1, Curtis School, O street near Wisconsin avenue; Station No. 2, Wilson Normal School, 11th and Harvard streets; Station No. 3, Webster School, 10th and H streets, and station 4, Van Ness School, 4th and M Streets Southeast.

Any one reporting a case of influenza within his resident zone will be sure of instant attention.

They are too busy at any of these stations to talk about the work, but one official at the Webster headquarters, recognizing the necessity of acquainting those who are willing to help but who do not know just how to go about it, took breath to say that anyone needing information should come right to headquarters or to any station most convenient, and that they would do the rest.

States emergent needs.

"What we need is helpers and more helpers; women who can make things easier by being around. Any woman can give a dose of medicine according to the doctor's orders, or straighten a pillow or pour out a bit of milk or whatever the needs of a patient call for-just as she would do in her own home.

It isn't much and yet it is everything. Naturally there are many women whose duties prevent their lending a hand. No reasonable person would expect it of her, but there are others. And it is those others that we are asking, begging, imploring to come and help."

The pestilence of Buddha's time is buried under the mold of ages, but his voice calls out today to men and women of Washington: "All men served their stricken brothers save those who deserve not the name of man."

This article shares a unique and maybe obvious solution to the problem of bodies and caskets piling up in some areas of Camden County, New Jersey.

Evening Public Ledger, Philadelphia, Pennsylvania
October 9, 1918

Prisoners dig graves

Sent from Camden jail to help relieve funeral stress.

Six prisoners have been sent from the Camden County jail to assist in digging of graves at Evergreen and New Camden Cemeteries to prevent delays for funeral processions reaching the cemeteries with victims of influenza and pneumonia. Including yesterday, 106 deaths from pneumonia and six from influenza had been listed at the City Hall, where burial permits are recorded, while records at the offices of the Board of Health showed 2405 cases reported by fifteen physicians, with thirty doctors yet to report.

Six prisoners have been sent from the Camden County jail to assist in digging of graves...

Cooper Hospital is filled with patients, and it has been planned to open another ward. The Homeopathic and the Municipal Hospitals also are crowded, while at the Emergency Hospital arrangements are being made for the opening of another ward on the first floor for the accommodation of about fifty more sick.

Through the co-operation of officials of the Victor Talking Machine Company twelve of the women employees at the plant who have had training have volunteered for work in the emergency ward at Cooper Hospital. They are to serve in three details of eight hours each, and their salaries will be paid by the company.

Chapter 6
THE NEW NORMAL

"On account of the influenza our office force was all shot to pieces last week..."

Oxford Eagle, Lafayette, Colorado, October 17, 1918

In a crisis, people do what they have to do. What may seem extraordinary at first, quickly becomes ordinary. Human resiliency and ability to adapt take center stage during these times.

The Spanish Influenza came in three waves: two in 1918 and one in 1919. The worst happened during the fall of 1918. Three phases spanning more than a year were enough to cause some people to change how they thought, lived, and reacted to their world.

This article describes a world where no coffins were available, and a husband who found a way to give his wife a dignified burial.

The Washington Times, Washington, DC
October 25, 1918

Builds coffin to bury own wife

Pottsville, Pa., Oct. 25.- No coffin to bury his loved one was the experience of a man living in Pottsville, after his wife had passed away a victim of influenza. He is a man with knowledge of handling tools, and in order to give his loved one a decent interment, he purchased the lumber for a coffin at a local lumberyard, and built the same to the best of his ability.

The question of procuring a coffin within his means was one that he could not properly meet and yet refuse to accept charity, hence, he took the above course and built a coffin to the best of his ability, then covered it with material that took away the thought of laying away the loved one in an indecent manner. It is thought that before the epidemic here is over many similar cases will be recorded in the country.

This article describes early attempts to keep people apart and establish a new routine among the citizens of a city. It was written on October 1, when it was obvious to many that the effect of the Spanish Influenza was about to get ugly. You can see that the recommendation then was the same as the recommendation today – stay away from other people.

**The Herald and News, Newberry, South Carolina
October 1, 1918**

The community in the grip of the Spanish Influenza

The Board of Health at a meeting on Saturday night ordered the churches closed and the pool rooms and the picture shows. It was scarcely necessary to promulgate an official order because nearly all business is temporarily suspended on account of the prevailing disease. We have heard of only a few serious cases and if the rules are observed not to congregate and to keep in the open air and to take your bed as soon as the disease overtakes you it is not so serious a matter. The only trouble the doctors say is the complications which follow the disease.

The thing is to do now is to live to yourself alone as far as it is possible while the disease is rampant in the land.

Let everyone do his part cheerfully and follow directions and it will all soon be over. No need to get alarmed.

Health Officer Player reported on Monday that he had placed quarantine on about 700 homes in the city.

The telegraph operator is laid up and no telegrams were received at Newbury Monday.

This article is very brief and contains some macabre humor. The incident took place as the Spanish Influenza pandemic was in its last stages. Fear of the disease, however, was still fresh in people's minds. Imagine the fear you might have felt if you had been sitting next to the body of your deceased loved one when the incident described in the article occurred.

The Daily Morning Oasis, Nogales, Arizona
December 11, 1918

Undertaker in flu mask comes near breaking up funeral

Friends of deceased make dash for doors when they see weird figures appear in masks.

Punxsutawney, Pa, December 10.- When the undertaker and his assistant went to the home of James Scarlatina, in Walton to take charge of the body of Mrs. Scarlatina who had died of influenza, they wore gowns and masks. Friends of the deceased immediately made a dash for the doors and windows, thinking that the spirits of the departed, with an escort had returned. It was with difficulty that the men convinced even the husband that they were mortals garbed to defeat the 'flu" germ.

This article gives another glimpse into the dramatic changes people experienced, including the helpless feeling that nothing they did made a difference as the disease continued to spread. It is interesting to note that all public gatherings were banned, except those considered essential for the war effort. The article also includes the new threat that anyone who disobeyed the draconian steps of isolation would be taken to court.

When a catastrophe is setting in, the boundaries of color and class tend to disappear, because people recognize that a disease is no respecter of persons. This article talks about wealthy people giving up their homes to help with the effort. Whether such deeds were voluntary or not isn't made clear. It does, however, drive home the point that, in the face of an invisible enemy, like Spanish Influenza, the things that normally matter take a back seat to security as our sense of safety diminishes.

The Bridgeport Times and Evening farmer, Bridgeport, Connecticut October 18, 1918

Drastic closing; Illinois means to combat "flu"

New Haven closes many additional places where crowds assemble - Waterbury establishes core of volunteer Health investigators. Scourge still growing toward peak in Connecticut.

Chicago, Oct. 18- Further drastic steps to check the spread of Spanish influenza in Illinois were taken last night when a proclamation was issued with the consent of the governor forbidding "all public gatherings of a social nature not absolutely essential to war work."

In making the proclamation the commission announced that there are 300,000 influenza cases in Illinois.

As influenza sweeps its way into all corners of the United States there is a distinctly increasing movement toward crowd suppression. In Waterbury previous closing orders were last night extended to saloons, drugstores, clubs and ice cream saloons be closed in so far as dispensing ice cream or drinks of any kind is concerned. Any person who violates this order will be haled into court.

Waterbury has raised volunteer health investigators, who will visit every home to bring aid, or to ascertain what conditions are.

Suffield has had 115 cases with six deaths, ten new cases were reported yesterday. Up to last night, 1,434 deaths had been reported to the state board of health, and 62,000 cases. About 48 per cent of the cases have been reported, and 65 per cent of the deaths.

New Haven till last night had 17 deaths of the disease, and the malady is just passing beyond its peak.

Acting in cooperation with the health authorities, Dwight Place church canceled three of its important meetings.

On account of the epidemic officers of the state teachers association have decided to postpone the state teachers conventions scheduled for October 25.

Community kitchen.

Manchester's latest assistance in fighting the epidemic is a community kitchen. In her trips around town, Miss Marion Tinker has found many families where there have been so many ill that there was no one to prepare meals. Miss Tinker has been doing much of this kind of work, but it was more than she could accomplish alone, but with the opening of the community kitchen yesterday and the Franklin school building much of this trouble was overcome. Meals were prepared for 25 families yesterday and after being placed in proper containers were taken around to the houses.

Washington, October 17.

The public health service now is actively directing the fight against Spanish influenza in 30 states in addition to the whole of Columbia. Particular attention is being given to providing nurses for the sick and supplying physicians for those communities where the doctors are unable to meet all calls made on them.

In spite of these and other measures taken by the public health service in co-operation with state and local authorities, the epidemic continues to spread in many sections. In others, however, particularly in parts of New England, it appears to have reached its crest. In a few states the number of new cases is showing decreases.

Continued improvements in conditions in army camps was shown by reports reaching the office of the surgeon-general of the army up to noon yesterday. New cases of influenza in all camps during the 24-hour period up to that time totaled 4,454 as against 5,668 the day before. Pneumonia cases decreased from 1,895 to 1,800 and the deaths were 684, a decrease from yesterday's total.

Calls of draftees undecided.

In discussing the improved conditions in army camps today, Secretary Baker said no time had been decided upon for beginning the induction of registrants into the camps. The military authorities now have the matter under consideration, he said, but they probably will fix no date until the epidemic has further subsided.

Reports on the influenza situation were received by the public health service today from 3 states. Most of these dealt with conditions as they existed several days ago and added little to new dispatches previously sent out from the states affected.

...Senate to appropriate $10,000,000 in addition to the $1,000,000 already provided by Congress.

To provide additional funds for fighting the epidemic, Senator Lewis of Illinois, yesterday introduced a bill in the Senate to appropriate $10,000,000 in addition to the $1,000,000 already provided by Congress. The money would be expended through the health departments of states and municipalities.

Because of the increased seriousness of the influenza epidemic in Washington, the supreme court yesterday announced that its recess, which was to have terminated next Monday, will be extended to Oct. 28.

Wealthy to give houses.

New York, Oct. 18. The residences of several wealthy New Yorkers will be opened tomorrow as convalescent homes for Spanish Influenza patients. Dr. Royal S. Copeland, Health Commissioner, announced last night. Vacant houses also have been obtained for use as convalescent homes, Dr. Copeland said, and these will be fitted up and opened as fast as nurses and doctors can be provided for them.

Near end in Bay State.

Boston, Oct. 18.-All reports received at the office of the state department of health up to last night indicated that the influenza epidemic in this state was nearing its end. Reports of many new cases were received from western Massachusetts, but Dr. Eugene R. Kelly, State

Health Commissioner, said this had been expected because of the late start of the disease in that section. In the state as a whole there was a decrease of 80 in the deaths reported as compared with Wednesday, and new cases decreased by one-half.

Fewer cases in Hartford.

Hartford, Oct. 17.- Reports to the local board of health showed 196 new cases of influenza in Hartford yesterday, compared with 239 yesterday. No decrease in the number of deaths was noted, 15 being reported yesterday.

Money always plays a role in tragedy, whether it's in mitigation or recovery. This article describes how large amounts of money were being spent to manage the needs caused by the pandemic.

In our modern world where debt and spending have lost some of their meaning, this may not seem important. But from 1916-1920, the national debt increased by nearly 8 times, which was extremely excessive in the eyes of the public. The war effort, however, was largely to blame for this deficit because the federal government was selling bonds to fund the war.

This article also mentions how some people questioned the constitutionality of the draconian demands made by the government, requiring individuals to behave in a certain way.

The Seattle Star, Seattle Washington
December 28, 1918

Flu costs million a day in the U.S.

New York, Dec. 28. –"Flu" is costing the United States nearly a million dollars a day!

Here are conservative estimates, based on a death roll of no more than 100,000 due directly to influenza and a sick role of no more than 2,000,000 in four months:

Funerals	$ 1,000,000
Doctors' fees	$16,000,000
Nurse bills	$16,000,000
Drug bills	$ 8,000,000
Lost to workers	$24,000,000
Lost to business	$48,000,000
	$113,000,000

More than $28,000,000 a month!

Flu quarantines prove unpopular

These estimates are undoubtedly under rather than over the facts.

They emphasize the vital necessity of stamping out "flu."

"Flu" bands are unpopular.

They hurt business intend to alarm the people.

New York's health officer, Dr. R. S. Copeland, opposes quarantines as a method for checking spread of "flu."

Los Angeles Christian Scientists refuse to obey a city ordinance closing their churches during "flu" epidemic. Judge White decided the law was unconstitutional.

San Diego and San Francisco tried making everybody wear a "flu mask." But the plan didn't seem to stop "flu," while it did make a lot of people wrathful.

Pittsburgh reports vaccination of 50,000 employees of Frick Steel Works with a vaccine prepared by Dr. E. C. Rosenow, University of Minnesota. Four cases of "flu" developed among the vaccinated.

Spraying nose and throat daily with good disinfectants prevents infection in many cases.

Health Officer Max C. Starkloff of St. Louis, Mo., is using the Rosenow vaccine as a preventative treatment and claims a high degree of success.

Surgeon General Rupert Blue urges formation of local committees everywhere to deal with outbreaks of the disease.

Such committees divide localities into districts, make house-to-house visitations, instruct the people in sanitary and preventative methods of fighting the disease, provide nurses and doctors and take such other measures as are deemed wise.

Prevention work is helping check the disease.

Spraying nose and throat daily with good disinfectants prevents infection in many cases.

Dr. E. R. Kelly, of Boston, claims some success with a blood serum. It is used in a hospital in Chelsea, Mass.

The New York Medical Record prints reports that injections of quinine under the skin have cured many victims of pneumonia following "flu."

It is believed that, with public and medical action, "flu" will be under control before winter ends.

But it may be an all-winter fight.

This is a fascinating article regarding the Spanish Influenza in Arizona. The fact that one fourth of the population had contracted the disease would strike fear in the heart of anyone at the time. Desperation and a search for hope became normal feelings in everyone's lives. This article includes another element that distressed an already desperate community: a report of people contracting the disease who had no contact with the outside world.

You may have noticed that the word "flu" was rarely used during this time. When it was used in newspaper articles, it was often put in quotes as in the following headline: The complete word, "Influenza" was generally the word that was used.

The word "influenza" and "influence" have a similar origin. Hundreds of years ago, it was believed that diseases were literally influenced by heaven or the atmosphere since there was no discernible earthly source for the malady. That idea may have meant something to the people in this article who could not understand how a disconnected group could have contracted the disease.

**The Copper Era and Morenci Leader, Clifton, Arizona
November 15, 1918.**

"Flu" situation is talk throughout state by doctors

That, with the observance of the strictest sanitary regulations, the epidemic of Spanish Influenza might be brought under sufficient control to warrant opening schools, churches and theatres on Monday, November 25th, was the opinion expressed by noon. The meeting was held in the governor's office at Phoenix with Gov. Hunt acting as chairman.

After a brief introduction by the governor in which he gave the physicians of the state much praise for their heroic service in the fight against the epidemic, Dr. O. H. Brown, state health officer, gave detailed account of his campaign for health in northern Arizona, describing the vaccine which was evolved at the local laboratory and the success with which it had been used.

Following Dr. Brown, at the request of the governor for a general discussion, Dr. John H. Lacey of Globe and Miami told of the ravages of the disease in that district. He said that one fourth of the population had had the disease; that four or five per cent had died. He said that the pneumonia cases following influenza there had been about 27 per cent mortality. He mentioned the extremely peculiar character of the pneumonia.

Expressing himself strongly in favor of vaccine, Dr. H. P. Mills, bacteriologist of the pathological laboratory here, told of his study of the bacteria and said that he was very much opposed to lifting the quarantine.

Dr. Allan Williams and Dr. A. J. McIntyre of Phoenix describe the success they had obtained with vaccine and recommended the establishment of free vaccine stations in Phoenix as had been done in other parts of the state.

As an illustration of how swiftly the epidemic descended upon Flagstaff, Dr. H. K. Wilson of that city told how the Flagstaff boys of the Normal football team had gone to Winslow to play the high school and about 20 girls had gone to attend a dance that night. Two days afterward the 11 boys and 20 girls were down with influenza and only about 18 out of the 220 persons living in dormitories of the school appeared to be immune and did not contract the disease.

...the pneumonia cases following influenza there had been about 27 per cent mortality.

Another interesting story of how the epidemic got its start in an Arizona town was told by Dr. W. F. Brown of St Johns. He said that a blind Mexican of St Johns played for a dance at Winslow one night and a few days afterward came to him to ask for medicine for a bad cold. Dr. Brown advised him to go home and go to bed. A few days later the man died. Dr. Brown warned the Mexicans to stay away from the place where the blind man lived, but disregarding his advice, about a hundred of them held a " pow-wow" there with the result that all contracted the disease in a virulent form and only a few recovered. As Dr. Brown himself caught the disease and there were no other doctors available, the situation in St. Johns was very desperate for several weeks. There was but one nurse for over 400 sick Mexicans and about 50 American patients.

Dr. Brown expressed himself as of the opinion that there was not much immunity in vaccine, but that there was more safety in masks, properly used, in isolation and strict quarantine. For the cure of the malady he had found that the main points were to keep the patient warm, in a well ventilated room and not to overfeed.

As county attorney of Gila county, C. N. Foster told of the strenuous efforts that have been taken to combat the disease there, with an expense of $25,000, for which there was no fund in the county treasury. He advised that hereafter counties be authorized to levy a small tax for just such an emergency as this. He told how the streets of Miami and Globe had been sprinkled with a disinfectant and chloride of lime used freely in the gutters.

Foster told a peculiar story in connection with the spread of the "flu" in his county. A family living ten miles out of Hayden in an isolated spot, which had not been visited or seen by anyone in over two weeks, caught the disease, the mother and five children all coming down with the disease at the same time.

...keep the patient warm, in a well ventilated room and not to overfeed.

The advisability of retaining a strict quarantine and requesting parents to teach their children at home was also expressed by Foster.

Prof. Loper, chairman of the central chapter of the Red Cross, described the work being done here and in other towns of the valley in establishing emergency hospitals. Speaking of the public schools he said he hoped that it would be possible to bring the epidemic under control soon and open the schools and that the pool halls and picture shows would not be opened until sometime afterward. He thought that schools would probably be able to make up several weeks at the close of the term.

That Morenci had endured an exactly similar epidemic last spring was the interesting information volunteered by Dr. L. A. W. Burtch of Clifton. Dr. Jeffries of Williams gave statistics of the epidemic at Williams, showing a very low mortality record.

Dr. W. W. Wilkinson of Phoenix declared that he believed that if adults and children were vaccinated the disease would soon be brought under control and the quarantine lifted in a fortnight.

This article is a warning about moving out of quarantine to a normal life too quickly. In this mountain city in Colorado, it took only one week out of quarantine before the numbers of ill were going up again.

It goes on to say that all gatherings were forbidden and, interestingly, the article actually says that two people constituted a gathering. In a barber shop, there could only be two people: the barber and the client. And the barber had to wear a mask.

This article also includes one of the most common elements seen in "Spanish Influenza" newspaper articles at the time – lists of people. Our modern-day concern about privacy was seemingly not shared by the people in 1918. Newspapers across the country often listed the following: names of citizens, their addresses, how they were doing, who was taking care of them, and how the illness was impacting them and their families. What you read below was typical of what you might see in newspapers across the country.

The Idaho Springs Siftings-News, Idaho Springs, Colorado
November 29, 1918

Influenza pays return visit to Clear Creek CO.

Cases more numerous but not so serious as first siege. Doctors rushed; nurses scarce

More genuine alarm seems to attend the raging of our second flare-up of influenza than was caused by the first, though, perhaps because of greater experience of all concerned, the various cases with a few exceptions do not seem so severe as during the former siege. Friday afternoon of last week there were but two known cases in the city. Now there are more than 100.

The ban enforced to prevent the spread of the first epidemic was lifted just one week, and then clamped down tighter than ever last Saturday evening. Two people constitute a gathering, and all gatherings of any sort are prohibited.

One man in the chair and one waiting are all that may occupy a barber shop. The barber must wear a mask.

In restaurants, patrons may occupy only alternating chairs, and during the rush of business, (whenever that is (?)), eaters are seated with difficulty. They are not compelled to mask, but if the trouble continues they may have to eat through a straw neatly perforating a mask.

The big sing prepared for Thanksgiving was of course postponed.

Some say the ban was raised too early while others think the schools should be open now as the safest place for children. Some think the new trouble was brought in after our own cases had about recovered. At any rate the distracting disease is with us again, and is deadly contagious.

> *Two people constitute a gathering, and all gatherings of any sort are prohibited.*

J. J. Hoban died Friday morning after a brief illness from heart trouble superinduced by Influenza.

Six members of the Ritter family are ill, all doing well except George, the sixteen year-old son, whose case was far advanced before the disease was recognized and a physician called. He has been very ill, and for some days his recovery has been considered doubtful.

Dr. Fred Weber was called to care for the Ritter family, and took an intense interest in the case, Dr. Mary Weber assisting. Mrs. Charles Long, a graduate nurse, was called on the cases, and all three are now ill at the Weber home, in charge of Mr. Long.

Miss Grace Curnow is recovering nicely from an attack. Little Virginia Ritter is ill at the Curnow home, and is better. Miss Bernadyn Marihugh, feeling exempt at least for a time because of her own recent severe case, is assisting in the Curnow home.

Misses Agnes and Marie Cribbis have had attacks not especially severe. Miss Agnes is nearly well.

Miss Anita Cruse came home last Friday from her school at Akron and has since been quite ill but is better.

The card had been removed from the Horsch home, and Frank is able to be about. But Miss Eula and nurse, Mrs. Hill, have suffered severe attacks in the past week, but are both on the road to recovery.

Miss Syvilla Mitchell came home from Freeland, and she, Miss Verda Rouse and little Marian are ill at the Rouse home.

Mr. and Mrs. Archie Palmateer were to go to Nunn, Colorado, to take charge of a ranch Thursday, but the flu intercepted their plans. They and their little son Clayton are all sick, but improving.

Mrs. Hefferman and two sons are ill.

Bennett Huffsmith, Ed and Billie Traylor are ill in the same house.

E. L. Siekmann is recovering nicely.

Eleven members of the Bob Wright family are sick, and all doing well.

Six are sick in the Robertson family, and are recovering.

Mrs. Harry Cooper and sister, Mrs. Benson of Denver are getting better.

Mr. and Mrs. Billig are quarantined. Miss Myrtle Huddleston is caring for them.

Two cases are reported in the Brunswick rooming house.

A sign has been placed on the Winkels home.

Bennie Bronson has it.

Mrs. Bronson, Mrs. Keogh and Harold Wiley on Chicago Creek are all ill.

Ray Enyeart is doing nicely.

Albert McColl, George Cruse, Charles Heller and Dick Mollard are all suffering with infleunza.

G. W. Ford is recovering. Mrs. Leland Leach is ill at the home of her parents, Mr. and Mrs. S. Florine.

Mrs. Dick Hull was reported ill Friday.

Will Mudge is a late case.

Al Roberts is recovering nicely.

Fred Blackmer has experienced one of the most serious attacks, but is now doing nicely. His brother Ted, however, is suffering a relapse, and his condition is critical. Mrs. Blackmer, and Miss Violet Robinson, who is with the Blackmers, are able to be up. At the Pascoe home three are ill, two at the Woodleys, two at Irvin's, four at Libby's two at Rogers', and nine of the Storms family are down or recovering.

Mrs. Schoellkopf is better.

Mrs. Nelson is well, but her daughter Esther is not recovering satisfactorily.

Mr. Allender, the baker at Roberts, came home from Denver a bridegroom last Friday, and has become a victim of the flu since, his bride becoming his nurse.

A little boy has it at the home of the widow Clark up near the reservoir.

Ed Griffin is a new case.

Harry (Ducky) Menzimer has been ill with the flu this week but is recovering in good shape.

The spread of the disease is such as to leave the impression that it is much more contagious than has been generally conceded. People will do well to not only stay apart, but to take all known precaution of a sanitary nature.

I had to stop and read this article when I saw the headline. The article validates something heard frequently during the COVID-19 lockdown: People in the entertainment industry will be put out. Interestingly, that same concern was described in newspapers during the Spanish Influenza pandemic. This article tells the story of a touring group of performers suddenly losing their jobs and being stuck in a town far from home.

**The Ogden Standard, Ogden, Utah
October 16, 1918**

Midgets are ill and one is in serious condition

Leo Stringer, the manager of Stringer's Midgets who were to have appeared at the Orpheum here last week, is having his hands full of trouble on account of the influenza epidemic. Five of his little and loyal band of entertainers are down with the malady, and one of them is this morning very sick Indeed.

"Jim," who is known to the company as one of their best and energetic stage hands, was overcome by an attack of heart failure in the Red livery barn where the ponies and the elephant make their home. Due to the ready ministry of Mrs. Miller and the stage carpenter, Sam Boardman, Jim was restored and thought he would be over his trouble in a short time. It was impossible to find a doctor in town at the time of this collapse owing to the fact that all the medical men in the city were out on their calls.

Mr. Stringer says he is willing to stay in Ogden five months, if that will mean the complete restoration of every member of his troupe.

This article was inset in another article and the headline grabbed me. It is doubtful there was any threat or physical coercion involved here, but the sense of desperation is obvious in the story.

Evening Public Ledger ,Philadelphia, Pennsylvania
October 9, 1918

Nurses are "kidnapped," so great is demand

Nurses are being kidnapped, so great is the demand for their services on influenza patients.

Just as she left a case on which she had been engaged a nurse was approached yesterday by a man who put her into a taxicab and whirled her away to his home, offering her any salary to nurse his wife.

The Visiting Nurse Society has had several of its nurses waylaid on their way home at night and taken to spend half the night ministering to sufferers in their neighborhoods.

This next article is quite long, but it gives you a broad and unsettling glimpse into what people were experiencing on a daily basis: ambulances and cars driving the sick, funerals, exhaustion, smells of antiseptic, requests for volunteers, sick children, the possibility of military patrol, closed businesses, and no public gatherings.

Evening Journal, Wilmington, Delaware
October 3, 1918

Disease epidemic hangs like pall over the city; Five are dead in one block; 100 deaths reported

Entire families stricken with influenza. Doctors unable to care for all patients and countless numbers of new victims reported as plague continues unchecked. City officials among sufferers. All public houses closed. Military patrol talked of

The Spanish influenza has fallen like a black pall upon Wilmington, numbering its victims by the uncounted thousands, with the death rate increasing by leaps and bounds, with every place of public gathering closed and silent, with a sobered and anxious population.

Ambulances and taxi-cabs are running day and night, doctors and nurses are almost in a state of collapse from physical exhaustion and cannot handle all the cases they have.

Doctors are utterly unable to tabulate their records to the Board of Health, because of pressing demands for every instant of their time from seriously ill people. Every minute brings new calls, every hour sees additional hundreds of persons prostrated by the contagion. The people of this city are warned not to take any chances of contracting the disease with its menace of pneumonia.

There have been 100 deaths from Spanish influenza and pneumonia reported to the Board of Health since Monday and others are expected today.

So numerous are the deaths that gravediggers find it impossible to open graves in time for the funerals. One funeral had to be deferred yesterday because of this reason.

There were five deaths at the Wilmington Country Club Emergency Hospital last night. There are more than 100 cases now in that hospital, and the patients are coming in so fast that the nurses this morning had no time to make a statement of the conditions there. A physician who had been on his feet all day attended patients at the country club last night stated that there were at least fifteen patients there who would not be alive when he made his next visit.

> ...so numerous are the deaths that gravediggers find it impossible to open graves in time for the funerals.

The Delaware road train leaving for down the State soon after 10 o'clock yesterday morning, was one hour late and departing from French street station, because of the delay caused by the shipping of numerous bodies, influenza and pneumonia victims. There were so many caskets at French street station that the pall-bearers were forced to act as porters and help the undertakers put the caskets on the train. One undertaker had 17 bodies, and another had 19 bodies to handle yesterday.

Whole families ill.

Among those reported dead to the Board of Health are John Green, colored, No. 203 1/2 Poplar street; John Thomas, No. 107 Shipley Street, John Lafeul, No. 328 East Fourth street.

Adam Pollock, No. 812 Taylor street, with his wife and three children were reported seriously ill last night. Pollock had paid the last $12 he had received from his wages for house rent.

At No. 805 Church street, a man, his wife, and seven children were reported seriously ill last night. The Board of Health is receiving scores of other reports of seriously sick persons so fast that they cannot begin to keep track of them.

Patrolmen Warren, Cary and Burns, were reported down sick with influenza this morning, making twenty-four police officers that are now off duty, sick and greatly handicapping the police department.

James H. Morris, a member of Local Exemption Board, No. 2, is confined to his home with influenza. W. F. Anderson, city building inspector, has the disease. The city offices are depleted, so many of their working force are victims of the contagion. A brother of Patrolman Rodenheizer died this morning. He was an employee of the traction company, and lived on Ferris street.

There were 44 patients in the New Century Club this noon, several of them pneumonia cases. Beyond the one death recorded there yesterday, no other fatalities have occurred there, and none of the present patients are dangerously low. This hospital is for shipworkers, and is in charge of the Emergency Fleet Corporation.

The Physicians' and Surgeons' Hospital has half a dozen nurses sick, and a number of influenza cases. The cases from the Homeopathic and Delaware Hospitals have been taken to the Country Club.

Mrs. T. C. DuPont nurses chauffeur.

Mrs. T. Coleman DuPont is acting as an influenza nurse. Her chauffeur was stricken with the malady, and no nurse being procurable, Mrs. DuPont promptly went to work to nurse the sick man. The doctors hope her example will be followed by other Wilmington women, whose services are urgently needed in this time of distress.

Dr. L. Heisler Ball made ninety calls and drove 200 miles yesterday, answering influenza calls in the district about Marshallton.

School girl dies.

Juanita M. Wright, aged 17 years, daughter of Mr. and Mrs. Robert E. Wright, of Rockland, died yesterday of pneumonia following an attack of the "flu." She was a member of B-3 Class of the Wilmington High School. The funeral will be held at 3 o'clock Saturday afternoon, and internment made in Silverbrook Cemetery.

The Board of Health is allowing ice cream manufacturers to dispose of all the ice cream they have on hand at present, but no new supply may be manufactured. The dealers will have to make this disposal upon their premises.

Whole streets are afflicted on the East side, and the disease has developed into a virulent type. Where one person in the family has come down with the disease, the others, as a rule, take it.

The Red Cross Motor Corps, which is working day and night, found five people dead in one block, and every house for two blocks had patients.

The need of women to make pneumonia jackets at the old City Hall headquarters is increasingly great. No women are permitted to work there who have an influenza patient in their houses. All other work has been set aside at the City Hall, to make hundreds of these jackets at once.

Military patrol likely.

The soldiers of the Twelfth Battalion, now on guard duty in the city, have been offered to the Board of Health to do patrol service, but up to this noon, they have not been called upon.

> *...dispose of all the ice cream they have on hand at present...*

The employees of the Majestic and Queen Theaters, whose services have been given by the theater proprietors, have gone to the Country Club to set up new cots, and otherwise help in checking the epidemic.

If the epidemic continues to increase, other emergency hospitals will be needed. Places now under discussion by the health authorities are the practically completed annex of the Mullin building at Sixth and King streets, Turn Hall and the Hammond Laundry.

Close State Hospital.

Trustees of the Delaware State Hospital for the Insane at Farnhurst at a meeting held today decided to close the institution to visitors indefinitely. There are a number of cases of "flu" among the inmates, but to date there have been no deaths as a result of that disease.

The Board of Health will meet at 5 o'clock this afternoon, to go thoroughly over the epidemic situation.

Don't spit on sidewalks.

The number of people on the city streets is notably less than usual, today. A number of careless people were noticed spitting on the sidewalks this morning. They could not use any means to increase the epidemic more quickly through the city.

Five months ago two Mormon friends, John B. Wallace and Jesse Hayes, each with a wife and child, traveled east 3000 miles from their home in Salt Lake City, Utah, to find new homes. Today both men lie dead, victims of influenza.

Wallace died at 6 o'clock last night at the John S. Thomas apartments, at 606 King street, where both families resided, and Hayes passed away at the New Century Club hospital at 8 o'clock.

Both Wallace and Hayes were boilermakers and were employed at Harland's.

Fifty per cent of the force of clerks are down with the disease in two of the largest offices of the Pennsylvania Railroad Company.

The health authorities yesterday also adopted a resolution expressing the thanks of the department to the DuPont Powder Company, the Wilmington Country Club, the Red Cross and the various hospitals for their hearty co-operation in the present outbreak.

The New Castle County Hospital today reported no deaths, but thirteen patients among the sick railroad employees in the emergency hospital there, and two new cases sent by the Bethlehem Steel Company.

Harry Baldwin, who is awaiting a hearing on a charge of forgery was found to be ill with the disease at the police station yesterday afternoon. He was removed to the emergency hospital.

> *Carbolic acid and other disinfectants have been sprinkled around stores and offices...*

Two other prisoners at the police station showed signs of being affected today. They are being held until a physician has examined them.

The old City Hall was thoroughly fumigated today, and no persons exposed to contagion will be allowed to enter the place. This will make it safe for pneumonia jacket workers. All the Red Cross auxiliaries, which meet in churches, schools, or clubs, and the Broome street branch, have been closed for the present. The Business Women's Auxiliary will not meet tonight in the Queen Theater Ballroom, nor until further notice.

Carbolic acid and other disinfectants have been sprinkled around stores and offices very generally throughout the city.

The Delaware Red Cross announced this noon that no Red Cross supplies would be sent out to auxiliaries or individual workers, or received at the old City Hall, during the epidemic. This means the practical suspension of Red Cross war work for the time being. The knitting, hospital supply, and baby layette departments at the old City Hall have been closed until further notice. The surgical dressings department will be kept open for epidemic emergency work only, chiefly making pneumonia jackets. The building has been fumigated from top to bottom. Everyone who enters will have to give assurance of non-exposure to contagion at home.

The death rate from influenza and pneumonia has so increased that the undertakers, who are short-handed, find themselves overwhelmed with shipping of bodies and burials. They, too, are applying for volunteer helpers.

Not enough physicians.

Physicians in Wilmington and its vicinity are being run off their feet by demands upon them to treat Spanish influenza victims. Many of them are refusing to take new cases because they already have as many as they can handle by working night and day.

In consequence, many persons who have influenza victims in their families are almost crazed because of their inability to obtain prompt medical aid.

Others complained bitterly that, because of the Fuel Administrator's order, for early closing, many drug stores are closed at night and it is impossible to obtain drugs. The State Council of Defense may be asked to take cognizance of this drugstore situation and also of the shortage of the supply of quinine in Wilmington. It is cited by one complaint that a man who had three influenza prescriptions to be filled walked from Twelfth and Popular streets to below Fourth and Market streets before he could find a drug store open to fill them so that he might take the medicine home to the suffering members of his family. In one drug store the service was refused on the ground that the Fuel Administration had ordered the place closed. Even the pleading of an official of the Wilmington Council of Defense failed to move the man in charge. He refused positively to fill the prescriptions.

The Board of Health has notified all city drugstores that the government early closing order has been suspended in regard to drug stores during the period of the epidemic. The drug stores are authorized to keep open as late as they wish.

Imperative demand for nurses.

Dr. Robert E Ellegood, president of the Board of Health, stated late last night that there was an imperative demand for more nurses to take charge of the increasing number of cases of influenza. He wished to make an appeal to all who could help in any possible way, either as nurses or assistants, to volunteer their services at once.

Miss Marie T. Lockwood, superintendent of the Visiting Nurses' Association in this city, is kept busy looking after the many poor victims of influenza. Two of her nurses are on the sick list and others cannot be had. Thus Miss Lockwood is forced to make many personal visits a day in addition to keeping in touch with the work of her assistants. In many families there are five and six down with influenza, and it is taxing the resources of the association to make even partial provisions for those in need. Miss Lockwood reports the situation as serious. In some places in the city, there are blocks in which the disease is to be found in every house. The percentage of cases of pneumonia is large.

...there are blocks in which the disease is to be found in every house.

Following the closing order issued by the Board of Health yesterday noon, barred doors and explanatory signs greeted the incoming theater crowds. The pleasure-seekers turned away with a sudden realization of the gravity of the situation. The "Little Teacher" company at The Playhouse, and the vaudeville actors at the Garrick have given but two of the expected week's performances. Movie heroes and heroines stare disconsolately from billboards at the crowds who are barred from patronizing them.

4,000 schoolchildren ill.

Dr. Clifford J. Scott, superintendent of city schools, sent out the word at noon to dismiss the schools. The schools began so late this year, owing to the need for labor, that the children do not welcome the enforced vacation. It is a regrettable handicap to an already difficult school situation, but a necessary one. Thirty public school teachers and four thousand school children already are sick with grippe, colds, and influenza.

As a result of the order near 12,000 children are affected in the public schools and 370 teachers while the 31 buildings will be closed.

Dr. Scott said that the Board of Health was to be commended for the manner in which it has handled the situation, and stated that the course taken was the only wise one.

The Rt. Rev. John J. Monaghan, Bishop of the Wilmington Diocese, stated that the Catholic clergy and teachers would follow out every decree and help to stamp out the disease as quickly as possible.

Including the two Catholic High Schools, 13 parochial school buildings are closed, affecting 3500 pupils and 150 teachers.

The Friends' School closed Tuesday. Five of the teachers are sick with influenza.

The drug stores are as busy as the doctors. When it was found that crowds of people were seeking medicine for the influenza long after the closing hours, the Government order for early closing hours was suspended in the case of drug stores. They will remain open every evening as late as they find it necessary during the epidemic. The supply of the medicines most in demand ran low or gave out entirely in many of the stores last night. Rush orders have been sent for more of the needed drugs.

The trolley cars smell like a doctor's office, as nearly everyone is using some preventive or curative antiseptic stuff. The cars are more comfortable to ride in than for many an autumn season as the conductors have received strict orders to keep the cars filled with fresh air.

The trolley cars smell like a doctor's office...

The change of temperature to warmer weather is a welcome help in combating the influenza, which requires both warmth and fresh air in its treatment. Men who report with high temperatures at any of the industrial plants are being ordered home at once. The city is now fully awake to the dangers of the epidemic and both individually and as a municipality is taking every means to check the spread of the influenza. One doctor has suggested that a person who must be exposed to contagion from the sick should put a piece of gauze saturated with an antiseptic solution over his nose and mouth when going into the sickroom, as a precautionary measure.

Churches to stay closed.

Unless a miracle of healing happens, Sunday will be "Don't go to church Sunday." There will be ninety-eight churches, Catholic and Protestant, closed on Sunday and week-days. Closing the churches has cancelled many entertainments and club meetings which were to be held in them.

The Delaware College ambulance was put into service last night. The two Phoenix ambulances, the New Castle County Hospital ambulance, the Federal ambulance from the guards' barracks, and the college ambulance have been making trips all day at top speed, without a pause, carrying "flu" patients. One of the commonest sights in Wilmington just now is an ambulance dashing frantically up the street. They worked all last night.

A half dozen dance halls and quite a large number of bowling alleys are closed because of the order.

The soldiers of the Twelfth Battalion, stationed in this city, have been offered for patrol duty, in certain affected districts, if such steps should be considered necessary.

During yesterday several men who had discovered that they had "a temperature" walked to the New Century Club building and reported themselves as patients. Others were taken there in automobiles and ambulances.

Owing to the large number of deaths due directly or indirectly to the influenza local undertakers are finding it difficult to handle all the victims.

Though no official figures have been announced, obituary notices in local papers are proof positive of the alarming number of deaths due to influenza.

Twenty-five per cent of the operating force at the Wilmington telephone exchange are on the sick list and the service is correspondingly crippled.

Of all users of telephones would confine themselves only to calls of actual importance...

In view of this situation, it has been suggested by those who are giving their time, energy and knowledge to combat the epidemic of influenza that users of telephones would help with the work by reducing the number of their telephone calls. In other words, great assistance can be given by all telephone users cutting out unnecessary and purely personal calls.

As conditions are now, there are many important calls delayed because the operators are engaged in connecting where conversation is of no importance. If all users of telephones would confine themselves only to calls of actual importance and really necessary it would relieve the strain upon the operators at the exchange. It is imperative that calls for physicians and nurses should not be delayed.

There were several applicants at the Delaware Hospital dispensary yesterday to take the inoculation treatment of the anti-influenza serum. The physicians at the hospital have faith in it and all of them have been treated, as well as the nurses. The preparation is made by one of the best firms dealing in medical supplies, a guarantee of its purity. The process is simple and there are no after-effects or reactions. The patient simply reels two or three pricks in the arm as though made by a needle. That is all. Four treatments are given at intervals of two days.

The hours set for treatment at the hospital are from 8 to 9 o'clock in the morning and from 5 to 6 o'clock in the evening. Dr. Emel Mayerberg is the physician in charge.

The saloons closed at 7 o'clock last night, with the exception of a few. All the retail liquor places including hotel bars are closed today. The order affects 167 saloons and bars.

The wholesale liquor houses are not affected by the order, as they are not congregating places; the liquor not being allowed to be drunk on the premises. Several such houses, however, were closed today.

The Non-Partisan League today offered to the Board of Health its rooms at No. 504 Market street, as an emergency hospital.

Councilman Cathcart of the Twelfth ward has offered his services to the Board of Health while the disease-epidemic prevails.

This final article didn't have a headline; it was a short note to the readers posted on the side column of the fourth page of the Oxford Eagle in Lafayette, Colorado. It gives an abbreviated look into a business trying to survive and maintain customers during a time when people were sick, employees were being pulled away for other responsibilities, and companies were being slowed down through no fault of their own.

Oxford Eagle, Lafayette, Colorado
October 17, 1918

On account of the influenza our office force was all shot to pieces last week and the Eagle was short of its usual amount of reading matter, but we did manage to get the paper out on time. This week conditions are a little better, but our force is somewhat disorganized yet. We ask our readers to be as liberal as possible, as we are doing the best we can under existing conditions.

Chapter 7

HUMANITY BY THE NUMBERS

"...the normal death rate has increased from two to seven times..."

Williston Graphic, Williston, North Dakota, October 31, 1918

In the world of pain and death, statistics are a morbid, albeit necessary tool. They tend to take the humanity out of the equation. Just like history often covers centuries in single sentences, the story of the Spanish Influenza pandemic is told the same way. The individual is lost in the midst of the statistics.

No one knows the total number of deaths caused by the Spanish Influenza, but it was over 50 million. It is estimated that it may have been as high as 100 million. It's a quantity that we can barely comprehend. To put it in perspective, if 100 million people in the United States were suddenly gone, we would lose about one out of every three people we know.

Perhaps the most troubling statistic is the flu "death toll" compared to the World War I "death toll." Approximately 675,000 Americans died of the Spanish Influenza while just over 50,000 were killed in combat.

It seems our real enemy is often not what we think it is.

However troubling it may be for us to reduce the death of millions of people to a dehumanized statistic, elements of that dehumanization existed in the midst of the confusion. For example, the first deaths were most likely very somber! But as the days and weeks progressed, the careful accounting of names and times gave way to piling bodies in hallways and alleys, and preparing people to be taken away as dead before they had drawn their last breath.

This first article is one of many examples of a frightened people watching death numbers increasing by the day.

The Washington Herald, Washington, DC
October 11, 1918

72 fatalities are recorded in grip plague.

District and federal agencies unite to fight epidemic.

Peril grows grave.

Red Cross organizes new unit to fight epidemic.

With every resource of the District and the United States organized to check the ravages of the influenza epidemic, the disease reaped a harvest of seventy-two lives in the city of Washington in the twenty-four-hour period between 9 o'clock Wednesday evening and 9 o'clock last night.

This is the greatest number of deaths in a twenty-four-hour period yet reported to the local health officers since the epidemic first appeared in the city.

With the number of deaths advancing at an alarming rate, the number of new cases in the District also grows during each succeeding day. Yesterday, 1,701 new cases of the disease were reported at the local office, 335 more than on the previous day.

Serious aspects discussed.

1,701 new cases of the disease were reported at the local office...

District Health Officer Fowler does not believe that the disease has even reached its climax-the city has yet to face the most serious stage of the epidemic. How soon the country may hope for relief the authorities do not attempt to say-they cannot even give out any hope the end will be reached for at least six weeks.

One of the most serious aspects of the situation, Dr. Fowler stated yesterday, is the inability of the local cemeteries to care for the dead.

A delegation from the Undertakers' Association called upon Dr. Fowler yesterday afternoon and asked that he take some action to assist them. It was stated that in one graveyard the vaults had a capacity to care for only thirty-five bodies. At present there are twenty some victims of the epidemic waiting burial in these vaults, and the cemetery superintendent declares more than ten funerals are scheduled to take place this morning.

In the other cemeteries the situation is almost as serious. The cemetery authorities cannot find laborers to dig the graves, and the bodies must remain in the vaults until the graves can be prepared. These vaults are rapidly being taxed to their utmost capacity.

Gravediggers needed.

Gravediggers must be found. Dr. Fowler declared yesterday that any man capable of doing the work would be doing the greatest public service to offer his services at once either to the superintendent of any of the cemeteries or by applying to Dr. Fowler at the District Building.

Although the numbers in this article are incomplete, in December the author already understood the statistical comparison between the deaths caused by World War I and the deaths caused by the Spanish Influenza. The article was written as the disease was slowing down.

The Daily Star - Mirror, Moscow, Idaho
December 10, 1918

Influenza kills six times as many as war

Calculations made by the national health officials at Washington indicate that influenza and resulting pneumonia have killed between 300,000 to 350,000 people in the United States since September 15. The entire death role of our overseas armies, from the time the first men landed until a few days ago, was only 53,000. Influenza has taken six times as many American lives as have been taken by war. An impalpable foe has swept away more American lives than have all the death-dealing agencies of the German army.

Reports of war correspondents picturing the placid contempt of death and danger shown by civilian populations in the battle areas have filled us with amazement. It seems incredible that untrained civilians could so school themselves to peril. But the same people who wonder at the self-possession of French and Belgian people when under fire have schooled themselves already to reckless disregard of even greater though less spectacular peril. They flock to the places of public assemblage where the darts of the invisible enemy are known to be thickest. After the first little flutter of fear they forget prudence and walk calmly into needless dangers. So hard it is to wean us away from our accustomed avocations and our pursuit of pleasure and entertainment.

- Spokesman review

I found this article particularly fascinating because it shows the actual rise in average mortality rates in specific locations. You will also notice that they estimated the disease would ultimately kill around 200,000 people across the country - a figure that was far exceeded in the end.

Williston Graphic, Williston, North Dakota
October 31, 1918

Scourge takes heavy toll

Epidemic of Spanish influenza now sweeping country worst in 40 years.

That the influenza epidemic which is now sweeping the country is the most disastrous known in this country in 40 years is shown by the figures just made public by the United States Census bureau, covering the principal cities of the country, which showed that the normal death rate has increased from two to seven times as a direct result of the disease.

Fall River, Mass. shows the highest advance. In this city the mortality has risen from an average rate of 13.7 per 1,000 people to 100.4. In Philadelphia the rate is 92.2 compared with a normal rate of 14.3. The rate for Washington has climbed from 15.5 to 86.7. Nashville, Tenn., has advanced from 11 to 78.6 and Baltimore from 15.6 to 65.5. The normal rate of New York and Chicago trebled during the epidemic.

...the normal death rate has increased from two to seven times....

The total of cases throughout the country since the disease became prevalent in the middle of September will run into millions. This is made evident by actual figures of the army camps. There have been hundreds of thousands of cases among the troops in training and while the death rate is not high, the number of fatalities is greater than the casualties in France.

Dr. Woods Hutchinson of Boston, noted writer on health topics, and who has been employed by the social insurance commission of California as an expert to lead in the social insurance fight in that state, states that in his opinion influenza will cause 200,000 deaths throughout the country before it is abated.

While the epidemic has practically abated in the east, it is sweeping westward and there is scarcely a community in the country which is not affected.

This article was written as the worst of the Spanish Influenza was darkening the country. The first two paragraphs arrested me. One of the statistics was taken from noon until 9:00 p.m. in Washington D.C. During that time, 425 new cases were reported. The overall number, which would reach into the thousands, had already begun.

The Washington Times, Washington, DC
October 9, 1918

Forty deaths here in day from influenza epidemic

1,722 new cases reported in last twenty-four hours.

5,176 cases since Saturday.

Peak of plague not yet reached.

Forty deaths among the civil population of Washington from the Spanish influenza epidemic were reported to the District Health Department in the twenty-four hours ended at noon today. This is the second largest number of deaths reported in any twenty-four hours since the epidemic started.

New cases reported between 9 o'clock last night and noon today number 1,297. New cases reported between noon yesterday and 9 o'clock last night number 425, making the total number of new cases reported in the twenty-four hours ended at noon today 1,722.

A total of 5,176 new cases have been reported since Saturday, and Health Department officials say this does not represent the entire scope of the epidemic in Washington.

Peak not reached.

Dr. William C. Fowler, District health officer, today stated that the epidemic still is on the increase.

"The number of new cases reported still is increasing," said Dr. Fowler. "I cannot predict when the epidemic will reach its worst stage."

The epidemic has not yet even reached a peak, according to Dr. J. W. Schereschewsky, assistant surgeon general of the Public Health Service.

"We will know within two or three days whether the epidemic is to be kept under control by the methods now in force, or whether much more drastic restrictions must be enforced," he said.

All meetings barred.

All outdoor public gatherings must be discontinued in the district. A formal order to this effect will be issued late today by Commissioner Brownlow.

> *No funerals or weddings will be permitted in churches, and no outdoor gatherings will be allowed.*

"This order includes all indoor and outdoor services in churches," Commissioner Brownlow said. "No funerals or weddings will be permitted in churches, and no outdoor gatherings will be allowed. This means the discontinuance of all Liberty Loan meetings. Therefore, I ask the people of Washington to buy more bonds. Don't let this epidemic lessen our bond sales."

Seventy-five die in day at Meade.

The epidemic caused the deaths of seventy-five more soldiers in Camp Meade in the last twenty-four hours. A total of 289 new cases of pneumonia and of 166 new cases of Spanish influenza is reported for the last twenty-four hours.

The disease claimed the life of another Washington soldier today at Camp Meade. Capt. Edward C. Cissel, of Company E, Seventeenth Infantry regiment died of pneumonia following influenza.

Depleted staffs at Washington hospitals today are coping with one of the most arduous tasks ever imposed upon local institutions.

Two Physicians succumb.

Two physicians and twelve nurses at the Emergency Hospital are suffering from influenza and the staff is depleted 15 per cent. Dr. Noble B. Barnes and Dr. Charles King, members of the surgical staff of Casualty Hospital, were stricken with influenza last night and five trained nurses also are suffering from the disease.

Thirteen nurses at Georgetown Hospital are influenza victims, and the nursing staff there is depleted by more than 10 per cent. The hospital reported 45 new cases of influenza today.

The Homeopathic Hospital today reports 14 nurses suffering from influenza, and an increase of more than 50 per cent in the number of patients admitted to the hospital.

Two more nurses became ill today at the George Washington University Hospital, making a total of 16 nurses suffering from influenza.

Chapter 8
SEARCHING FOR ANSWERS

"..take the secretions from the noses and throats of influenza patients and place them in the noses and throats of the volunteers..."

New York Tribune, New York, New York, May 25, 1919

The study of viruses was in its infancy in the early twentieth century. By 1918 it would still be years before the electron microscope would make the complex structures of a virus visible. But people clearly understood that illnesses like the flu were passed from person to person in close proximity. In a desperate attempt to control the spread of the illness, public meetings were banned, churches were closed, and funerals were limited to family members. Some cities made sneezing without covering your mouth illegal, and some communities went as far as telling everyone to stay in their homes for an extended period. These rules were clearly difficult to enforce, so out of desperation, citizens often took matters into their own hands when they would see people violating them.

It is impossible for us to understand the mindset of the people at the time. It's important for us to remember just how different our world is now than it was in 1918. If nothing else, we have considerably more information and understanding. And as the saying goes, "The truth shall make you free." Simply understanding the illness seems to make a big difference in human psychology, even if there is no cure. But for the people of that time, treating diseases was little more than a guessing game, as you will see in these newspaper articles.

From a health standpoint, the world was considerably more frightening than it is today. The limited success of various cures and health tools exacerbated people's fears of disease and sickness. During times of a pandemic, desperation set in and people tried anything to stay healthy or regain their health. Many people alive during the Spanish influenza in 1918 had lived through the pandemic that hit the world in 1889, less than three decades earlier. The fear of that horrible experience was most likely lurking in the minds of many who were now nearly thirty years older.

Although the people in 1918 were slightly more advanced technologically than people in 1889, they were the children and grandchildren of people who lived in the 1800s. I think it's safe to say the people in the 1800s had more in common with people that lived 5,000 years ago than they do with us today.

To put it in perspective, when you had children in the 1800s, you expected at least one of them to die before reaching adulthood. It was actually common for people to lose many of their children. People would often give their next child the name of a child they lost to death previously. And it was also common for at least one parent to die before all of the children had reached adulthood. The parents, grandparents, great-grandparents, etc. of the people in 1918 came from that world. So even with the advancing technology, education and scientific breakthroughs, we can understand the desperation and thought process that had carried over from previous generations.

This first article from South Carolina references something called Wampole's Formolid which was an antiseptic solution.

Edgefield Advisor, Edgefield, South Carolina
October 30, 1918

Mr. Thurmond gives effective remedy for influenza.

Mr. Editor:

The prevalence of influenza has prompted me to make enquiry of the best physicians for the most effective preventatives of said disease, and the following remedies may or may not prove beneficial in any particular case, but I am informed that the remedies below given are now in high favor at least in some of the army camps and medical men of high standing recommend them, I give them for what they are worth, to wit:

Teaspoon level full of ordinary cooking soda, three times a day - reduce quantity for children.

Gargle throat and flush nasal tubes with warm soda or salt water three or four times a day; however, Wampole's Formolid or some other germicide is preferable to the soda or salt water. Of course contact with the disease should be avoided, if possible. The germs causing this disease are said to create an acid poison, which is neutralized by soda.

If you contract the disease go to bed at once and call a physician.

J. Wm. Thurmond.

Early twentieth century advertising in newspapers was often spattered with health potions and gadgets. The "Oxygenator," for example, was a small contraption you would sit by your window to force life-saving oxygen into your body through tubes that connected to your head and limbs. The "New Life" machine was a tool resembling a hair dryer that was said to improve blood flow and could help rheumatism, indigestion, headaches, gout, sleeplessness, kidney and bladder issues, and more. Numerous contraptions, medicines and elixirs were advertised in early twentieth century newspapers. Many of these items were sold as cure-alls.

Although it wasn't necessarily new to the market, during this same time Vick's Vaporub was being advertised as something that could help with the flu. Many of us remember having Vaporub smeared on our chest when we were sick as children.

This next article is little more than an advertisement for Vick's Vaporub. I included it here because it is fascinating to see something that still has a niche in the world of health over a century later, and for the same basic treatments.

In this article the product is being sold as a tool to keep airways open. The reason for this is obvious: many people didn't actually die from the flu, they died from pneumonia. They literally drowned in bloody liquid that built up in their lungs. So anything that kept the airways open seemed to be a critical component of survival. Where so many other medicine companies had cure-alls during this time, Vick's was honest in stating that there is no cure for the flu; it simply has to run its course.

To this day there is some question as to whether or not Vick's Vaporub actually does anything of value. In any case, it clearly gained a foothold in the world of treating the sick.

Notice that this article references the need to "stay perfectly quiet" as part of one's treatment. I found this recommendation in many articles from that era.

Forest City Press, Forest City, South Dakota
November 7, 1918

How to use Vick's VapoRub in treating Spanish Influenza

The influenza germs attack the lining of the air passages. When VapoRub is applied over throat and chest, the medicated vapors loosen the phlegm, open the air passages and stimulate the mucous membrane to throw off the germs.

In addition, VapoRub is absorbed through and stimulates the skin, attracting the blood to the surface and thus aids in reducing the congestion within.

CALL A PHYSICIAN – GO TO BED – STAY QUIET – DON'T WORRY

There is no occasion for panic - influenza itself has a very low percentage of fatalities. Not over one death out of every four hundred cases according to the N. C. Board of Health. The chief danger lies in complications arising, attacking principally patients in a run-down condition - those who don't go to bed soon enough, or those who get up too early.

Spanish Influenza, which appeared in Spain in May, has all the appearance of grip or la grippe, which has swept over the world in numerous epidemics as far back as history runs. Hippocrates refers to an epidemic in 412 B.C. which is regarded by many to have been influenza. Every century has had its attacks. Beginning with 1831, this country has had five epidemics, the last in 1889-1890.

The symptoms.

Grippe, or influenza, as it is now called, usually begins with a chill followed by aching, feverishness and sometimes nausea and dizziness, and a general feeling of weakness and depression. The temperature is from 100 to 104 and the fever usually lasts from three to five days. The germs attack the mucous membrane, or lining of the air passages - nose, throat, and bronchial tubes; there is usually a hard cough, especially bad at night, and frequently all the appearances of a severe head cold.

The treatment.

Go to bed at the first symptoms, not only for your own sake, but to avoid spreading the disease to others - take a purgative, eat plenty of nourishing food, remain perfectly quiet and don't worry. Quinine, aspirin or Dover's Powder, etc., may be administered by the physician's directions to relieve the aching. But there is no cure or specific for influenza - the disease must run its course. Nature herself will throw off the attack if only you keep up your strength. The chief danger lies in the complications which may arise. Influenza so weakens the bodily resistance that there is danger of pneumonia or bronchitis developing and sometimes inflammation of the middle ear, or heart affections. For these reasons, it is very important that the patient remain in bed until his strength returns - stay in bed at least two days or more after the fever has left you, or if you are over 50 or not strong, stay in bed four days or more according to the severity of the attack.

External applications.

In order to stimulate the lining of the air passages to throw off the grippe germs, to aid in loosening the phlegm and keeping the air passages open, thus making the breathing easier, Vick's VapoRub will be found effective. Hot wet towels should be applied over the throat, chest and back between the shoulder blades to open the pores. Then Vick's should be rubbed in over the parts until the skin is red, spread on thickly and cover with two thicknesses of hot flannel cloths. Leave the clothing loose around the neck, as the heat of the body liberates the ingredients in the form of vapors. Those vapors, inhaled with each breath, carry the medication directly to the parts affected. At the same time, VapoRub is absorbed through and stimulates the skin attracting the blood to the surface and thus aids in relieving the congestion within.

So avoid persons having colds - which means avoiding crowds - common drinking cups, roller towels, etc.

How to avoid the disease.

Evidence seems to prove that this is a germ disease spread principally by human contact chiefly through coughing, sneezing or spitting. So avoid persons having colds - which means avoiding crowds - common drinking cups, roller towels, etc. Keep up your bodily strength by plenty of exercise in the open air and good food.

Keep free from colds.

Above all keep free from colds, as colds irritate the lining of the air passages and render them much better breeding places for the germs.

Use Vick's VapoRub at the very first sign of a cold. For a head cold, melt a little in a spoon and inhale the vapors, or better still, use Va-poRub in a Benzoin steam kettle. If this is not available use an ordinary tea-kettle. Fill half-full of boiling water, put in half a teaspoon of Va-poRub from time to time - keep the kettle just slowly boiling - inhale the steam arising.

Vick's VapoRub can be had in three sizes - 30c, 60c, $1.20 - at all druggists.

This article tells the lengths to which people would go to study this invisible enemy. It was a group of Naval volunteers who put themselves into a study that is absolutely repulsive. They were seen as heroes for allowing themselves to be involved in such a strange process.

In this article you will see that the volunteers understood that transmission of the flu virus took place through coughing and sneezing.

In other articles, they add a third form of transmission – spitting! It was clearly a common thing at the time – something we rarely see today.

This article was written just after the worst of the pandemic ended.

The Bamberg Herald, Bamberg, South Carolina
February 27, 1919

Influenza is a mystery.
So far it has defeated medical skill and science.
(By Frederick J. Haskin)

An experiment that makes the transmission of influenza a more baffling mystery than ever, and which at the same time places on record an act of self-sacrificing heroism by about 100 naval volunteers, has just been completed by officers of the United States public health service cooperating with medical officers of the United States Navy at Boston and San Francisco.

As nearly everyone knows, scientists all over the world, in combating the spread of influenza which is still going on, have proceeded on the assumption that it is transmitted chiefly by coughing and spitting. The theory has been that the diseased mucus thrown out by these acts is filled with the germs of influenza, which thus find lodgment in healthy tissue. All the experiments heretofore made seem to indicate strongly that influenza is transmitted in this way, and it is well accepted that most other respiratory diseases are so carried.

The latest experiment consisted in submitting the 100 men who volunteered for the purpose to every possible method of infection with influenza germs through the nose and throat. These men risked their lives for the general good, and for the advancement of science. They went through a singular trying and repulsive ordeal. They, and everyone else, believed that they were being inoculated with the dread disease which is destroying millions of lives all over the world. Their heroism is fully equal to that displayed some years ago by the men of the army medical army corps who exposed themselves in Cuba to the bites of mosquitoes in order to determine finally whether yellow fever was transmitted by that insect. The only difference in the two experiments was in the result. Some of the officers who exposed themselves to the bite of the mosquito contracted yellow fever, and one of them died, thereby establishing the soundness of their theory. The volunteers who submitted themselves to inoculation with the germs of influenza were fully expected to take the disease, and were prepared to die. But not one of them developed any symptoms of influenza.

> ...100 men who volunteered for the purpose to every possible method of infection with influenza germs through the nose and throat.

This astonishing negative result, which is the sensation of the day in scientific circles should not tempt anyone to be careless in the matter of coughing and spitting or in exposing himself to infection by those acts. As officials of the public health service point out, it may be that the germs of the disease disappear as soon as or immediately after the symptoms appear. Something like this is true of other diseases. In measles, for example, it has been found that the germs which cause the disease are all gone within five or six days after the appearance of the rash, and the case is no longer contagious. The discovery of this fact, which was made by Anderson and Goldberger of the public health service only a few years ago has led to shortening the quarantine for measles by more than half.

"These new experiments in the transmission of influenza," said Surgeon General Blue, "show how difficult is the influenza problem. They by no means indicate that we can afford to disregard coughing, sneezing and spitting as common means of spreading disease, and even in the case of influenza this source of infection should always be borne in mind. I believe however, that we have not paid sufficient attention to other paths of infection, especially to the lips, mouth and hands. The fact that the disease was much less common in army camps where the sterilization of all eating utensils and dishes was rigidly enforced, shows the importance of the mouth as an avenue of infection."

There can be no doubt that these experiments at Boston and San Francisco were carried out with the utmost thoroughness. Lieutenant Commander Rosenau of the navy medical corps and Surgeon Joseph Goldberger of the public health service were the officers in charge of the Boston experiment, which was made at the quarantine station on Gallop Island. Forty-seven men were the subjects of this part of the experiment. All of them had been more or less exposed to the disease and 39 of them had never had any bronchial disease. This means that some of them may have been naturally immune to influenza, but it is not at all probable that all of them were.

The first experiment consisted in thoroughly infecting the noses of about ten of the men with cultures of Pfeiffer's influenza bacillus, of virulent germ commonly found in influenza. None of the men developed any symptoms. The next form of the experiment was to take the secretions from the noses and throats of influenza patients and place them in the noses and throats of the volunteers by means of swabs and sprays. The time occupied in removing the diseased mucus from a sick man and putting it into the nose and throat of a well man was reduced to as little as 30 seconds. Yet none of the men so infected developed any symptoms of the disease.

...secretions from the noses and throats of influenza patients and place them in the noses and throats of the volunteers...

Determined that the test should be exhaustive, the doctors next submitted a group of volunteers to infection by actual coughing and spitting. For this purpose ten volunteers were selected, and ten bed patients who had recently come down with severe attacks of influenza. Each of the volunteers leaned over the bed of each of the sick men, conversed with him for a few minutes, and allowed the patient to cough directly in his face, so that there should be no doubt of a transmission of diseased tissue. Each volunteer was thus exposed to ten different cases of influenza, and was in close proximity with them for not less than three-quarters of an hour. Yet not one of these volunteers developed any symptoms of influenza.

The experiments in San Francisco, which were carried out under the direction of Surgeon G. W. McCoy of the public health service and Lieutenant De Wayne Richey of the United States navy at the Angel Island quarantine station, were very similar in method and in result. The men who volunteered for these experiments had been vaccinated with Pfeiffer's influenza bacilli and pneumonia germs. If, as European reports would indicate, influenza is caused by an ultra microscopic germ, such vaccination would be without protection to those so vaccinated. None of these men had been exposed to the influenza epidemic.

In this experiment there was no direct exposure to patients, but the additional methods of infection were tried of injecting the blood of an influenza patient into that of a volunteer, and of introducing the pure cultures of influenza bacilli into a volunteer's eye. No one of these men developed influenza.

The result of this experiment has left the medical world completely bewildered.

The theory which has apparently been upset by these experiments was originated by a famous French physician Nicolle, who claimed to have produced influenza with a material obtained from mucus excretions. He produced the disease with this material after filtering through a fine porcelain filter, showing that a germ was present which was not only too small to be detected with the microscope, but too small even to be held back by the fine pores of unglazed porcelain. Foster, an American army surgeon, showed that common colds were produced by equally minute germs. The work of Foster bore so directly on the problems presented by influenza that it may be said to have led to the experiments there described.

The only thing which can be considered proved about influenza so far is that it is still a mystery both as to the nature of its causative germ and as to its means of transmission, and therefore especially dangerous. Authorities, however, still consider influenza a crowd disease, and all unnecessary gatherings of people should be discouraged when influenza is prevalent.

This next article describes a "mind over matter" approach to treating the disease. Although having the "right attitude of mind" may not cure the disease, it might help. How? Many people became so concerned about getting sick, they convinced themselves they were sick, and that helped clog the system. Keeping the public calm has always proved to be a critical element in dealing with any disaster.

**Audubon County Journal, Exira, Iowa
October 24, 1918**

Quit thinking about influenza

Des Moines, Oct. 14- A plea for the application of common sense and the basic principles of Christian Science to the present influenza epidemic was made by the "flu" committee Saturday. The immunity from infection enjoyed by the soldiers at Camp Dodge, who are Christian Scientists was brought to the attention of the committee by Marshall Miller, president of the Trades and Labor assembly. "These people are keeping themselves in good health by right attitude of mind," said Dr. W. C. Witte, chairman of the committee. Many people contract diseases mainly through fear of them, and this fear is the first thing we have to overcome in conquering the epidemic.

...people can think themselves into having a disease or even into their graves...

Power of thought

"There is no doubt in my mind that people can think themselves into having a disease or even into their graves, if they are not careful. I do not mean to make light of the situation in any way, for it is most certain a serious one, but instead of expecting to catch influenza, if people would use common sense and preventive measures, they would be less likely to contract it."

"Entirely too much publicity has been given the symptoms," said H. W. Byers, corporation counsel, "and this had a bad effect on the people. I think preventive measures should be given out instead."

Asked whether Christian Scientists of the city had objected to the quarantine, Dr. Witte replied: "Most certainly not. I have found in all my work that the scientists are always quickest to comply with any suggestion of sanitation or the good health of the community."

With every book loaned at the city library, a printed slip giving measures which will prevent Spanish Influenza is given out, through the cooperation of Forrest B. Spaulding, city librarian.

The following article is almost laughable. One has to wonder if this was part of the misinformation campaign going on because of the war. Throughout the pandemic, the United States government was busy having fundraisers to sell Liberty Bonds to fund the war. They downplayed, and at times prevented, any news from being reported that might hurt the war effort. Today this article seems naïve at best.

Decorah Public Opinion, Decorah, Iowa
October 16, 1918

Says "flu" not germ disease

The epidemic is caused by atmospheric conditions is the theory of Dr. C. B. Spates of Des Moines

CERTAIN AMOUNT PREVAILS EVERY FALL AND WINTER

Says not to get overheated and permit yourself to cool quickly. Avoid drafts.

That the present epidemic of Spanish influenza is caused by unusual atmospheric conditions, especially favorable to its development, and not by a germ is the theory advanced by Dr. C. B. Spates of Des Moines in the Register.

Dr. Spates devotes much of his time to research work, and is somewhat of an independent thinker along lines of medicine.

"I can produce all the symptoms of Spanish "Flu" in a perfectly healthy individual at any time," declared the doctor, "and I will not use germ cultures for the purpose either. I would only need to direct him to perform some arduous form of labor which would profuse perspiration. Then I would ask him to sit down in a spot where he would cool off rapidly. He would have a bad case of influenza in no time, and if permitted to go unchecked, it would probably develop into pneumonia and end his life."

Dr. Spates says a certain amount of influenza prevails every fall and winter, identical with the disease now sweeping the country. The only features distinguishing the present scourge are its new name, its wide spread, its more than ordinary malignant character, and fact that it seems unusually inclined to develop into pneumonia. All these characteristics, except its name, he attributes to peculiar atmospheric conditions.

Speaking of the prevalence at the cantonments, the doctor says the conditions are more favorable for its breaking out than they are elsewhere.

"The boys are taken out and given hard training. They come in warm and perspiring from their physical exertions. Most of them cool off quickly. The surface of the body cools while the interior remains unusually warm. This leads to congestion, and they are taken with what would ordinarily be called a case of grip, but now is styled Spanish influenza.

"Unless their systems have resisting powers they would probably be taken with a cold under similar circumstances in any season. The present season, however, owing to the climatic conditions already referred to, the cold assumes a more severe form than usual and is more liable to bring on pneumonia."

> I can produce all the symptoms of Spanish "Flu" in a perfectly healthy individual at any time...

The precautions against taking the disease suggested by Dr. Spates are simple. There are certain nose sprays that are valuable, he says. For the most part, however, he advises that the ordinary precautions observed against colds will suffice to keep off the "flue."

"Don't get overheated and permit yourself to cool quickly. Avoid drafts. Breathe fresh air. Eat a sufficient amount of nourishing food. Keep your bodily functions up to par."

In this way you can keep the disease at bay. But don't let up on your precautions if you want to avoid being affected, he says.

With prohibition on the horizon in 1920, there were already "dry" communities across the nation. Interestingly, some people believed that alcohol could actually play a role in curing diseases like the flu. As a result, druggists were the only people who had it available. But as you will see in this article, when druggists were running low on alcohol, the police weren't!

Evening Star, Washington, DC
October 6, 1918

Whisky used to check spread of influenza

Prescribed by Alexandria physicians in conjunction with other remedies.

ALEXANDRIA, Va., October 5. - Whisky taken from "bootleggers" by state prohibition officers and members of the police force is being used to help to check the spread of Spanish influenza here.

Some physicians have recommended that whisky be taken in small quantities in hot water along with other medicine. This being a "dry" city it was impossible to obtain liquor. A few druggists only had whisky on hand and they, of course, had a license to sell it only on physicians' prescriptions. Their supply soon was exhausted.

Recognized as Emergency.

Owing to the extreme necessity of having whisky the authorities have turned over a certain quantity of the contraband liquor to the licensed druggists and this, of course, is given to customers only on prescriptions.

Today, however, the impression went around the city that persons suffering from the influenza could obtain whisky simply by applying at police headquarters. As a result the police were besieged with personal calls and also with calls over the telephone making inquiries as to how to obtain some of the confiscated liquor.

Erroneous Impression Corrected.

The police soon dispelled the illusion, informing inquirers that whisky for such cases could be obtained only on physicians' prescriptions from druggists having the required license to sell liquor.

This article was so fiery I had to include it in this book. An article such as this would be condemned in the United States today because it exudes a feeling of xenophobia. But as you will see from the article, there was a general feeling amongst Americans that many of the world's maladies came from Asia.

The writer not only has a fascinating theory as to why the Spanish Influenza ravaged the army so quickly, he also demonstrates the common understanding that it often wasn't the flu that killed people, it was the secondary illnesses.

New-York Tribune, New York, New York
May 25, 1919

Germ "explosions" that shook a continent

The influenza epidemic came out of Asia, where all the world plagues are hatched, and swept westward across the world, says medical writer.

I

The influenza epidemic has practically expired, but whence it came and whither it drifted, what its germ is and what it is not, and how it should and how it should not be treated are matters that even scientists are not in agreement upon.

Woods Hutchinson, the entertaining medico-journalist who sets forth technical subjects garbed in smooth flowing English, has contributed to "The Metropolitan" an article tending to show that the "flu" epidemic, as well as all other of "our great cosmic plagues," was generated in Asia and with winged feet followed Westward at the heels of civilization. It was born and-

"Like a thief in the night it glided past our quarantines and in eight short weeks carried death and wailing into five times as many homes as German gas and bullets and shells had in sixteen months. The Spanish 'flu' in less than two months brought our total losses up to more than half of England's entire toll of dead in four and a half years, covering all the Seven Seas and half the continents of the globe.

"Like others of our recent blessings, the flu came to us from Europe - but it wasn't Europe's fault; she just got it from Asia and passed it on to us. Nor did the war have anything to do with it except to delay its arrival on our shores, by making scarce westbound messengers to carry it. For the bacillus of Pfeiffer is a choice and particular traveler; it must be personally conducted - can only be carried by hand and delivered in person by cough or sneeze.

> ...it glided past our quarantines and in eight short weeks carried death and wailing into five times as many homes as German gas and bullets and shells...

"We call it the Spanish influenza because it didn't originate in Spain, which is no further from the fact than the names of a good many other diseases. Like all the other great waves of pestilence, which sweep across the globe at stately intervals, it began in Asia. In that great seething motherhive of unwashed and sweltering humanity are hatched and brewed all our great cosmic plagues. Smallpox, cholera, the black death or bubonic plague, pleuro-pneumonia, influenza, all stew and bubble there together constantly in that fetid melting pot of all the races and all the posterities, that ever-seething witch's cauldron of contagions. About once in thirty years the great pot boils over, and a seething, scalding wave of pestilence sweeps its scummy and blighting way across the whole western world.

II

"The flu is no new thing; in fact, like most of our diseases, the more we investigate its history and origins the more age-old and venerable does it become. It can be safely dated as far back as the sixteenth century and it is strongly probable that the famous and fatal English 'sweating sickness' of the fourteenth century was a form of influenza. There was a famous and historic outbreak of it in the first decade of the nineteenth century, during the Peninsular campaign, when Napoleon and his conqueror Wellington faced each other for the first time on the rugged plateaus of Spain. It put both armies out of business at once and drove them into winter quarters in the middle of the summer, and so furious was its onset and so swift its spread that the ignorant Spanish peasants said that it must be due to an 'influenza dal

Estrellas,' 'An influence from the Stars,' and 'influenza' it was called and has remained until the present day, because we didn't know any better, and according to some of our highbrow bacteriologists of the Brahmin caste don't yet.

"So that it was quite a curious instance of history repeating itself that the disease in this appearance should again have been called the 'Spanish flu,' though Spain was really no more to blame for it then than now. If the influenza happens to travel fastest overland, with the caravans, it reaches Europe by way of Russia first and is called the 'Russian influenza.' If it moves more swiftly along the water routes, up the Red Sea and the Suez Canal, through the Levant and along the Mediterranean it enters Europe by the Mediterranean ports, and is dubbed 'Italian' or 'Spanish flu.'

"What did the war have to do with the influenza? Contrary to very general popular impression, almost nothing at all except to markedly delay its westward spread. In ordinary times of peace we should have had half a million immigrants pouring westward in steady stream from Eastern and Southeastern Europe, carrying the influenza bacillus like flotsam upon its bosom.

The flu kitten had grown at a single bound into the pneumonia tiger, and proceeded swiftly to devastate and lay waste in every direction...

"The war even greatly retarded the spread of the plague across Europe, for, with the exception of the wounded and the soldiers going home on leave, most of the flow of human material was westward or against the spread. This is strictly shown by the fact that whereas the influenza had in former days developed a regular standard gait of its own, namely thirty to forty days from its announcement in Moscow before its arrival in Paris and London and thirty days more to New York. In 1918, it took ninety days from Moscow to London and ninety more from London to New York."

III

The epidemic flowed with the "ordinary streams of traffic" and was dependent upon persons as carriers. It developed what Dr. Hutchinson terms an "explosiveness" that was one of the marvels of the disease and a mystery as well, as he points out:

"The most dramatic and fateful enigma of the whole drama of pestilence was its sudden and mysterious increase in virulence and deadliness within a few weeks of its arrival in America. The pestilence entered the country at Commonwealth Pier in Boston through and in the bodies of sailors of the United States Navy returning from convoy duty with the transports in European waters. This was in the last week in August. By the first of September it had spread in scattering patches all through the suburbs of Boston and was piling up a total of nearly four thousand cases among the young Jackies in the Boston naval training district. On September 8 an 'explosion' of several hundred cases occurred at Camp Devens, which blazed up in the most furious and fatal epidemic of pestilence which this new world has ever seen, prostrating fourteen thousand five hundred of our soldier boys, causing seven thousand cases of pneumonia and over eight hundred deaths, in a population of about forty thousand, all inside of about two weeks. The flu kitten had grown at a single bound into the pneumonia tiger, and proceeded swiftly to devastate and lay waste in every direction, that the soldier boys in the cantonments, then the youth and manhood of the entire nation, until nearly half a million of our strongest and finest had been slaughtered.

"Something happened in Camp Devens to hatch or inflame Spanish influenza from little more than a cold in the head into a raging pestilence. What, or perhaps who, was it? There are several explanations, no one of them wholly convincing, probably all of them played a part in the catastrophe, and all alike scarcely creditable to the intelligence of the higher military command.

"The first and most plausible theory is that of the one age and one sex community. The population of the army camps or cantonments consists almost entirely of boys and young men between the ages of twenty and thirty. Now the spread of the influenza germ through an ordinary civilian community is of an uneven and broken character. The first case, say, is in a young man, and the germ adjusts itself to the chemical composition, the temperature and the resisting powers of his tissue. He passes it on to, perhaps, his mother, and here the germ must make a change of habit and adjust itself to a new type of soil and host. The mother transmits it to the father and again the germ has to adjust itself to a new environment. The father infects his little daughter and the little daughter in turn transfers the germ to the chilly and withered tissues of her grandmother or grandfather. Every success of host of the germ is a new and different country with a climate to which it must adjust itself. It can make no headway, gather no momentum.

"But let the germ once enter one corner of a community made up entirely of young men of the same age and under like physical conditions of food and lodging and occupation, all it has to do is to adjust itself to the conditions prevailing in the tissues of its first victim. And the rest is easy"

IV

So swift was the work of spreading the disease through army movement that "exactly thirty days from the date of the first 'explosion' on September 8 at Camp Devens the cantonments on the Pacific Coast had been reached and everything from American Lake, in Washington, in the north, to Camp Bowie, in Texas, and Gulfport, Louisiana, in the south, had been infected." In most instances there were from 5,000 to 8,000 cases and from 700 to 1,100 deaths, according to size.

The germ enters the nose and mouth and lodges in the cavities of the nostrils and back of the throat and larynx. "There it hatches or incubates from two to five days, until it has grown sufficiently strong and numerous to pour its toxins into and overwhelm the system."

One of the bitterest things in the whole tragedy is that the doctor has to simply stand and watch his patient drown...

Then – "the prostration comes on with headache, backache, and a high fever, running to 104 or 105 degrees, rapid pulse, hurried respiration and severe pains and chills. This goes on for from two to four days by which time in five-sixths of the cases the cells of the body get the upper hand of the invader, neutralize his poisons, or toxins, and figuratively speaking 'fire him out' or engulf him within the bodies of the white blood corpuscles. Then the high fever breaks, headache grows better and the patient begins to sit up and take notice.

"Four-fifths of the danger is now over and all the patient has to do is to gradually get well. But the situation is not so safe and sane as it looks for though the germs have disappeared from the nose and throat, they have gone down into the lungs, or windpipe and bronchial tubes. Here the fluids of the body usually overwhelm them and they're coughed up and got rid of, perhaps to lodge in someone else's throat and attack a fresh victim. But in about one-sixth of the cases the germs get the upper hand of the situation and begin an invasion of the walls of the bronchial tubes, causing congestion, inflammation, and hemorrhage which are due to their destructive effects upon the blood vessels. This results in tiny ulcers in the walls of the bronchial tubes and these may eat their way in until in some cases they reach and open into a blood vessel, when the patient has a hemorrhage from the lungs and fresh red clots are coughed up into the sputum cup which may even reach a pint or a pint and a half. In many cases the germs are swallowed and attack the coats of the stomach and intestines, producing hemorrhage from the bowels.

"Then the savage attack which the germs and their toxins make upon smaller blood vessels damages their walls so badly that the blood cannot longer circulate through the lungs, and we get a literal water-logging or dropsy, technically known as oedema, of various parts or in bad cases the whole of a lung and the luckless patient literally drowns in his own fluids. One of the bitterest things in the whole tragedy is that the doctor has to simply stand and watch his patient drown, which takes from one to three days, as powerless to do anything to help him as if he had had his hands tied behind him."

Chapter 9
HEROISM

"...five nurses of the Philadelphia General Hospital have died martyrs to duty."

Evening Public Ledger, Philadelphia, Pennsylvania, October 12, 1918

This chapter is titled "heroism" because there is an unmistakable undercurrent of hope and strength in all the articles. During times of fear, desperation and tragedy, many people recognize a higher call. Suddenly, people begin running toward the fire rather than away from it, and they become our heroes. It is fortunate for us that newspapers existed during the Spanish Influenza epidemic so the names of heroes, including their acts, could be permanently archived.

Some of them lost their lives because they helped others. Those who didn't die certainly knew death was a possibility. While reading the following articles, we might ask ourselves, "Would I be one of these people?"

Variations of the phrase, "refused to quit" are found in numerous stories in the articles I reviewed. Health professionals and volunteers burned themselves out in their quest to save lives, and that seemed to play a role in their own demise. The words "martyr" and "hero" are common in these stories.

Evening Public Ledger, Philadelphia, Pennsylvania, October 12, 1918

Five nurses die; martyrs to duty

54 ill of influenza at Philadelphia General Hospital

Refuse to quit work

Worn by long hours of brave fighting against the influenza, five nurses of the Philadelphia General Hospital have died martyrs to duty.

Fifty-four other nurses at the institution have been stricken with the malady. Several of them have contracted pneumonia and are in a critical condition.

The five nurse victims who gave their lives are Miss Nellie O'Neill, a head nurse; Miss Effie Ballain, a student nurse; Miss Mabel Bougher, head of the children's ward; Miss Marian Walter and Miss Myrtle M. Sides, both student nurses.

Narratives of the heroic manner in which the nurses are battling against the epidemic, refusing to leave their work in the wards caring for 1200 or more patients afflicted by the malady, despite the ravages of the disease and the fact that many of them are ill, was narrated today by William G. McAllister, the superintendent.

Director Krusen, health officer, has sent a call for fifty additional nurses to meet the emergency at the Philadelphia Hospital at the suggestion of Superintendent McAllister.

Praised for Devotion

"They are heroes-every one of them," said Superintendent McAllister. At that moment a white-caped figure came into his office to mournfully announce the death of Miss Sides, who passed away this morning.

Miss O'Neill and Miss Baltain died last night, while Miss Mabel Bougher succumbed on Tuesday and Miss Walter on Wednesday.

...refusing to leave their work in the wards caring for 1200 or more patients...

In each case the nurse refused to quit her post, although stricken, related the superintendent. Each continued to work day and night, helping the other victims brought into the hospital, hundreds of them, until practically carried away weak and helpless to the infirmary.

"No soldier on the field of war battle could be any more courageous," said Superintendent McAllister, "Nor are the nurses on the front one whit more heroines than these girls."

Fine Records of Victims

Miss O'Neill had been attached to the Philadelphia General Hospital for several years and made her home in this city. Miss Baltain was also a resident of Philadelphia, having come from Turkey, her birthplace, to study nursing in this city. Miss Bougher, who had charge of the children's hospital, was a Philadelphian.

Miss Sides came from Lancaster to this city to study at the Philadelphia Hospital, while Miss Walter, another student nurse, was one of the twenty young women sent to the hospital from Vassar College.

In chaotic situations, it is fascinating to see order rise out of disorder. In this article, the situation starts in a school building with a teacher and students. As the chaos of the pandemic sets in, the school building turns into a hospital, the teacher becomes a medical assistant, and the students are converted into medical helpers and cooks. In moments of crisis, people tend to create order in chaos. This article is a great example of that.

El Paso Harold, El Paso, Texas
October 19, 1918

Girls assist fighting 'flu'

Winslow domestic science class great help; preachers phone operators.

Winslow, Ariz., Oct. 19.- "I have become an enthusiastic advocate of domestic science in the schools since coming to Winslow," said Dr. Allan Williams, of Phoenix, a member of the state health service, who states that much of the success that has attended operation of the two school hospitals here has been due to their possession of well equipped kitchens.

...the domestic science teacher remained at her post, with a squad of high school girls, rendering diet kitchen service...

When the high school was commandeered for the reception of influenza patients, the domestic science teacher remained at her post, with a squad of high school girls, rendering diet kitchen service that has been of the greatest value.

Two preachers are acting as telephone operators at the main hospital and the sick are being brought in by the fire department truck, while the railroad agent is in charge of all transportation for the doctors, their patients and supplies.

State Health officer Brown is here in general charge of epidemic work in northern Arizona, the state being also represented by Vice-chairman Adams and Secretary Green of the State Council of Defense. Doctors and nurses have been brought from Phoenix, Los Angeles and other points and scattered wherever needed all the way eastward from Williams. All are overworked, but the worst is believed over.

Especially stricken was Gallup, N.M. On the Arizona line, the station of Navajo, with only 20 population, had 75 cases as refugees came from the ranch country around. Snowflake, a mere Village, has 200 sick. At Saint Johns a single nurse had 50 to care for. Most of the rural doctors had been called to war. At Springerville there had to be deputized a mailman who had studied medicine years ago, but who could follow instructions. The people generally are exact in their observance of the rules established for their safety, here calling daily at several streets spraying stations and avoiding handshaking and unnecessary contact with their fellows.

Nurses dying from the very illness they were fighting was all too common during the Spanish Influenza pandemic. This article is a story about one person who ultimately lost her life while assisting others.

Pullman Harold, Pullman, Washington
November 1, 1918

Gives life in effort to save sufferers

Miss Mary B. Packingham weakens constitution in heroic effort to save others and falls victim to influenza

The name of Miss Mary B. Packingham, registered nurse, located at Pullman for several years past, was Tuesday added to the long list of Influenza victims. Miss Packingham having passed away at the A. T. O. house hospital early Tuesday morning. The death of Miss Packingham, according to physicians and others in touch with the situation, was the indirect result of over-exertion and heroic self-sacrifice on her part in assisting in combating the epidemic which within a few days enveloped the entire city. Miss Packingham is known to have worked 36 hours at one time without rest, organizing the A. T. O. and church hospitals and at the same time serving as head nurse at the A. T. O. house.

...was the indirect result of over-exertion and heroic self-sacrifice on her part in assisting in combatting the epidemic...

With acute conditions accompanying the inability to secure an adequate staff of nurses at the outset of the epidemic, Miss Packingham labored faithfully to the limit of her endurance and when she was herself attacked with influenza her bodily strength was not sufficient to stand the strain, and pneumonia speedily developed, claiming her life within a few days.

Miss Packingham had followed her profession in Pullman for about 12 years, being for several years associated with the Pullman hospital. She had recently enlisted in the overseas service and was await-ing her call to military duty when the epidemic which resulted in her sudden demise made its appearance among the soldiers at the State College.

She is survived by her mother and two brothers, all residents of Illi-nois, and the remains have been shipped to Strandville, Ill.

In all the hundreds of local homes where Miss Packingham served as a nurse in cases of Illness she was beloved and honored and her sudden death caused a pall of sorrow to envelop the entire commu-nity. Determined to do her full part in the great struggle for Liber-ty, she enlisted for overseas nursing duties, but made the supreme sacrifice in the fight against the influenza epidemic before receiving her call. She has died the death of a hero, and her name should be enrolled with those of the soldier dead on the parchment of honor and self-sacrifice.

This is another example of a person giving up her comfort to help others through a tragedy. In this case, however, the person is not a nurse. She was the city editor of a local newspaper. She spent her spare time caring for those who needed assistance, beginning with her friends and ultimately her parents.

In the "note" section of my Introduction, I pointed out that type was placed by hand when printing newspapers in the early part of the twentieth century. As a result, editorial standards were much lower than they are today. For example, a person's name might be spelled differently in the same article. In the following write-up, you will see an example of this. Nelly Larson's name is spelled "Larson" in the heading and sub-heading and "Larsen" in the composition.

Williston graphic, Williston, North Dakota
October 31, 1918

Miss Larson succumbs

Nelly M. Larson passed away Friday after a brief struggle with pneumonia.

Was tireless worker and helping to nurse sick at outbreak of epidemic, funeral yesterday.

All Williston mourns the loss of Nellie M. Larsen, who answered the call to the Great Beyond Friday morning, October 25th, after a heroic struggle with pneumonia which caused her death after an illness of but six days.

A week before her death, Miss Larsen was apparently in the best of health, although worn in mind and body through her efforts to help and relieve the suffering caused by the influenza in Williston. In the week preceding her illness, she had labored with the sick, answering calls at all hours of the night, and uncomplainingly entering sick rooms where exposure meant almost certain contagion. But her thoughts were never of herself, and her greatest happiness was to see others made happy through her efforts.

The strain from the long night vigils at the bedside of influenza patients, and her tireless efforts to relieve their suffering, resulted in the breakdown of her own health, and when on Saturday, October 19th, she was taken ill, her natural strength had waned, and she was unable

to cope on even terms with the dread disease which claimed her.

After ministering to the needs of the sick in Williston, she went on Friday, October 18, to the home of her parents, 12 miles northwest of town, to nurse and assist them during the epidemic. But the strain of the work she had been doing was too much for even her strong body, and on Saturday she was stricken, and six days later she passed away.

Nothing was left undone by those to whom she was dear to see that she had every care and attention, and everything was done that was possible to save her life, but without avail. She made a heroic struggle to remain on this side of the Divide, but the Grim Reaper was the victor, and she died at 4 a. m. Friday morning.

The funeral services were held Wednesday afternoon from the Hamre Undertaking Parlors, and the remains were laid to rest in Bethlehem cemetery northwest of the city. Rev. Ferster conducted the services, and because of the decree of the health officials the funeral was private, only the closest friends and some of the family attending.

...answering calls at all hours of the night, and uncomplainingly entering sick rooms where exposure meant almost certain contagion.

Although only entering upon the threshold of life when she was called Beyond, Nellie Larsen had accomplished much for the good of the community and those among whom she lived. Born at Springfield, Minnesota, July 2, 1893, she came to North Dakota with her parents in 1906 and lived with them on their farm near Williston. Even when a young girl she was a tireless worker and no task on the farm seemed too great for her to accomplish. Naturally bright and intelligent, she finished the eighth grade at the rural school in Wildrose school district No. 34.

In 1909 she enrolled as a student in the Williston High School, and although handicapped by having to work her way, she completed the course in three years, and as valedictorian of her class. This record is unique in the history of the local school and will stand as a tribute to her efforts and ability.

After the completion of her high school work, Miss Larsen taught at school house No. 2 in Wildrose district No. 34 and made an exceptional record. Then she came to Williston and accepted a position with the Bruegger Mercantile Co., as bookkeeper and this she held for several years, resigning to take a position with E. R. Brownson.

In the spring of 1916 she entered the employ of The Herald, and for a year and a half had charge of the bookkeeping department. Then at the resignation of Glenn Townsend, to enter the military service, she stepped into the City Editor's position, which she filled with great credit to herself and the paper she served until her death.

Her parents, Mr. and Mrs. J. J. Larsen, and twelve brothers and sisters survive her. She was the second child in the family, and the first to pass away. All her family are here except her elder brother, William, who is with the American Expeditionary forces in France and a younger brother, Victor, who is with the U. S. Army at Nogales, Arizona.

As a member of the Congregational church, she was a tireless worker for all that was good. At one time she served as Secretary of the Sunday school.

Her position as city editor of The Herald brought her in contact with hundreds of people, and not one but speaks of her as a kind and true friend. The entire city receives with profound sorrow the tidings of her death, and her loss will be keenly felt. Her going reminds those who were fortunate enough to know her of the worth of her friendship and the joy of her companionship, which again, with renewed consciousness of loss, they lose.

Many people who were not in the medical field were looking for ways to help. One obvious way was to help nurses and doctors get from house to house and hospital to hospital. There are records of some doctors making upwards of 100 visits a day. In Washington DC, two people put together a "taxi" service that was operated on a volunteer basis. People volunteered their cars and their time each day to chauffeur medical professionals on their rounds. This volunteer group drove medical professionals to some 1,000 visits each day.

A photo of one of the directors of this service included the following quote: "I've got the best taxicab service in Washington, with the wives of bank presidents, admirals and millionaires serving as chauffeurs. My list of drivers reads like a social register."

The Washington Times, Washington, DC
October 26, 1918

Taxis that don't tax wage swift fight with "flu"

Taxicabs to anywhere at any time free, is the service offered by the newest and most modern taxi company in Washington which, each day, is answering over a thousand calls covering more than 5,000 miles of ground and employing over 150 chauffeurs and chauffeurettes.

This taxi cab service is run entirely by volunteers. Gasoline and oil is supplied by the government. All the automobiles were loaned by people in Washington to help fight the epidemic of Spanish influenza.

Meet the bosses.

This information comes from Lieutenant Howard S. Fisk of the Navy Pay Corps and Dr. Charles V. Herdliska of the Public Health Service, both of whom are president, vice president, secretary, manager, bookkeeper, and supply department of the Public Health Service Taxi Cab service. Headquarters are in the Webster School, Tenth and H streets Northwest.

Lieutenant Fisk says that no taxi service can beat this one.

Dr. Herdliska says that Washington is receiving a real treat.

How do they do it in war times? This is the question both Lieutenant Fisk and Dr. Herdliska say they can answer upon a moment's notice.

What Lieutenant Fisk says.

Here is what Lieutenant Fisk says about the taxi cab service and why it is better than any in Washington: "Our keynote is efficiency. Our capital - well, we have none. Our chauffeurs are men, women, boys and girls. We pay no salaries. We use over 150 different cars, roadsters, and nearly every make of car on the market. We are always ready. We run the only perfect service."

> *Our work is to carry more than 150 nurses and physicians to more than 1,000 addresses a day.*

Dr. Herdliska in addition to holding three or four executive positions in the taxi service, is also statistician. Here's what he says: "The whole secret of our service is that it is free. Our work is to carry more than 150 nurses and physicians to more than 1,000 addresses a day. To do this we need automobiles. We asked the public to lend us their cars and their chauffeurs or the cars themselves. They responded and we supplied them with gas and oil and organized our service. You see we are running this taxi cab service for the public health service. Our cause is worthy, also immediate. Persons in Washington suffering from the influenza need nurses and physicians, and need them quick.

1,000 cases a day.

We answer 1,000 calls each day. We carry more than 2,000 passengers each day. We use more than 600 gallons of gasoline each day. To hire taxicabs would cost us over $2,500 a day. We are proud of our service, but especially proud of our chauffeurs and cheufferettes. But still we need more cars.

Dr. Herdliska and Lieutenant Fisk have been working from 8 o'clock in the morning to midnight. They have been doing this for the past two weeks and will continue it until the epidemic wanes.

Here are a few of the figures Dr. Herdliska gives about the taxi service. It has made over 25,000 calls, 5,000 trips, covered over 100,000 miles, and has carried more than 40,000 passengers since its inception, several weeks ago.

There were two conflicts going on at the same time: World War I and the Pandemic War. Many girls spent their days working their war-related jobs, then running off in the evening to act as volunteer medical assistants. This article talks about one such person.

The Washington Times, Washington, DC
October 28, 1918

War workers give nights to nursing

A Government clerk during the day and an influenza nurse at night.

This is the latest record established by women war workers. The first war worker to volunteer her services as a nurse at night is Mrs. Eleanor Sanford, a rural mail clerk in the Postoffice Department.

When Mrs. Sanford closes her desk in the Government office after her day's work, she reports for duty at the Webster School, the headquarters of the Public Health Service. It is 4 o'clock then. She acts as volunteer nurse in emergency calls until midnight and is subject to call from her home until the wee hours of the morning.

Mrs. Sanford is one of scores of girl war workers to give their time after office hours to fight the influenza. Like Mrs. Sanford they give Uncle Sam seven hours day work and eight hours night work, making a fifteen-hour working day.

They report to Lieut. Howard S. Fisk in charge of transportation, at his office in the Webster School, and are assigned to a "case" when an emergency call comes in.

"I always wanted to be a nurse," said Mrs. Sanford. "I gained some practical experience when I was home with my mother. She was very delicate and the duty of nursing her fell upon me."

When you study newspaper articles about the Spanish Influenza, you see the words "Red Cross" almost everywhere. The words Red Cross were synonymous with nursing. The Red Cross, which had 107 local chapters in 1914, had grown to 3,864 chapters by 1918 when the Spanish Flu was at its worst. This army of 31 million adult and junior members played a critical role in caring for wounded soldiers and those sick with Spanish Influenza.

The Washington Times, Washington, DC
October 9, 1918

Women enlist to battle with grip

In France when a man rushes into the face of death with never a care for his own welfare, they give him the Croix de Guerre. But, right here in Washington, women are volunteering to nurse influenza patients without hope of reward other than that which comes with knowledge of a duty performed. From the moment that the Red Cross, The District Health Department, and the United States Public Health Service sent out their appeals for volunteer workers, a constant stream of willing women have presented themselves at the newly opened recruiting station in the old Commercial Bank building 14 and F streets Northwest. Many have had little experience, just that which comes to the average woman and taking care of her own family, but all are eager to serve in whatever capacity the Red Cross thinks best.

Miss Fanny F. Clement, herself a Red Cross nurse, is in charge of the recruiting of these women. More than 50 presented themselves at her desk today. All seem to have but one idea: they want to be of service.

Many offer to go into the homes and do the housework and take care of the children in cases where the mother is prostrated with the influenza. They realize the nature of the disease and its deadly infectiousness. They know that nurses and even doctors exposed to the disease have contracted it and have died of it.

None of these facts deters them.

Some are women of wealth, others have only moderate means. All seem to want to prove that the American woman never fails nor flinches when the emergency calls.

All will be equipped with the sanitary masks and every precaution will be taken to protect them while they are at work. Miss Clement wants everyone to feel that every sort of service is needed and appreciated: someone to run errands, someone else to drive a car and take the nurses and supplies to places where they are needed. Willing hands and a good heart being just as much in demand as expert services.

> *All seem to want to prove that the American woman never fails nor flinches when the emergency calls.*

Army Nurse dies of grip as she attends soldier victims here.

Dead in the service of her country, Miss Lillian Aubert, one of those upon whom the government had depended to help check the spread of influenza in Army hospitals and camps was buried today from the Walter Reed hospital. No member of that brave and indefatigable band of women who make up the personnel of the Army Nurses' Corps had worked more earnestly than Miss Aubert. Coming here from the Philippines where she served in the Army hospital, she was to have been head nurse in charge of the soldiers afflicted with the disease.

She contracted influenza last Thursday. Pneumonia followed and death resulted Monday afternoon. Although only 30 years of age, Miss Aubert was the oldest member in point of service of the Army Nurses' Corps.

This article describes another fascinating way the Red Cross was utilized during the Spanish Influenza epidemic: the group was called the Women's Motor Corps of the Red Cross. I included this article because it shows that people who want to help will find a way. When you are part of an organization you normally look to the organization for direction, support, materials, etc. On the other hand, a truly motivated person finds a way to complete a task even when the resources aren't available. I am including this article as an example of how people will give you the shirt off their back, or as in this case, the bedding off their bed.

The Cordova Daily Times, Cordova, Alaska
December 27, 1918

Women's motor corps fights flu epidemic

Denver, Dec 27: The women's motor corps of the Red Cross did heroic work in fighting the epidemic of Spanish influenza in Denver, many members often giving assistance to victims of the malady up to the moment when they were stricken themselves.

One of the self-imposed duties of the corps was the distribution of gallons of soup made by the National League for Women's Service. In many instances members of the corps have gone into sick rooms to serve patients. Cases of dire need have been discovered by them. In instances where they found entire families ill and often without sufficient bedding they have collected these articles from their own homes and from friends.

Members of the corps also used their cars in carrying patients to hospitals.

In addition to sharing more about the Red Cross, this article stands out as an example of pure humanity. It's the story of a woman with no training in health care volunteering to use the abilities she has to help others.

The Daily Gate City and Constitution Democrat, Keokuk, Iowa, October 22, 1918

Women in the epidemic

Women in other cities, where the Influenza situation is not so safe as here, are carrying soup and other food to stricken households.

The women in Omaha and in Chicago and in Quincy are doing volunteer nursing as well as making soup at community kitchens.

A former Keokuk woman now living in Omaha, drives a car every day for a settlement worker who distributes soup and gives nursing service from house to house.

The public health nurses are doing valiant service in stricken cities, but untrained women are doing volunteer service.

A Keokuk woman was in Winnetka, Ill, when the influenza epidemic broke out there. She is a local Red Cross worker and was interested in the health situation and so rode about a half day with the superintendent of public health nursing. She said every woman in that fashionable suburb was at work. One woman, a painter of miniatures, came to the public health office and said, "I can't nurse. I haven't any talent for that, but I can cook and I've come to volunteer for that." She was accepted to do that work and as long as she is needed she will do invalid cooking for the patients at the improvised hospital in the most exclusive country club in Winnetka.

The spirit of the times calls for service and the women as well as the men are meeting it heroically, as a matter of course, but with no show of heroics.

This was one of the most poignant examples of a person giving his life for the cause of fighting the pandemic. It describes the best of humanity – a person who has no particular training but is willing to do whatever he can to help others, even complete strangers.

As the article states, no one knew much about this man. He was relatively new to the community and lived alone. He had no family in town and volunteered his service because he didn't have anyone dependent on him. Even knowing the danger he was in, he still sacrificed his life to help others.

**Morris Tribune, Morris, Minnesota,
November 1, 1918**

Fred Pott loses life helping others

The death of Fred H. Pott occurred Tuesday night and his body was buried Thursday morning. It can truthfully be said that Mr. Pott gave his life serving others and he is entitled to all the honor and praise that can be bestowed on his memory.

When the influenza epidemic broke out in this locality, he went to the Linsley home and took care of Homer Linsley until he died. From there he went to the Martin Anderson home, where every member in the family was sick, and he nursed them as best he could and also took care of the stock and did the chores. He stayed there until after Mr. Anderson and son Gaylord died and then he had to return to his home to rest up. He was taken sick last Friday with influenza and although everything possible was done for him he passed away Tuesday. He was to have been brought to the hospital in Morris Tuesday but he was too sick to be moved. His life could not be saved, but through his efforts other members of the Anderson family were brought back to good health.

That he gave his life for humanity, there is no question...

Inasmuch as he served the Anderson's so well, his body was laid to rest in the same lot with Mr. Anderson and son.

Very little is known of Mr. Pott in this locality. He came to Morris about four years ago with Henry Bergherr and was a stranger to Mr. Bergherr at that time. For a year, he and Mr. Bergherr farmed together and the next year Mr. Pott moved on to a farm near the Aug. Huebner place, where he made his home ever since. He was a bachelor and lived alone.

It is thought that his parents live in New Haven, Mo., and a letter was found in his pockets, which he had just received from his brother, Herman, at that place. He was notified by wire of his brother's death but the funeral arrangements were made at once as no public funerals are allowed and the State Board of Health insists that influenza victims be buried at once. Mr. Putnam of Morris wrote a very nice letter to Herman Pott telling him of the noble service his brother had rendered and told of how well he was liked here, having made nothing but friends since coming to Morris four years ago.

A short service was held at the cemetery for Mr. Pott, Reverend Pilgrim officiating.

The last time that Mr. Pott was in Morris he said that he was going out to care for the people suffering with influenza, as he felt it his duty. He said he had no one dependent on him and he realized how much he could do for those in need. That he gave his life for humanity, there is no question, and his name will go down in history as one who did a real service for his fellow men.

Chapter 10
FINAL THOUGHTS

"So hard it is to wean us away from our accustomed avocations and our pursuit of pleasure and entertainment."

The Daily Star - Mirror, Moscow, Idaho, December 10, 1918

However different our world is today from 1918 - and it is indeed different - the basics for dealing with a pandemic haven't changed much. Although we can define and understand viruses and bodily processes more thoroughly today, we are still just as vulnerable to a world-wide outbreak as we were in 1918.

We should consider ourselves lucky that we have a relatively well-documented pandemic from our recent past. We can observe the successes and failures of those who survived that pandemic and hopefully navigate future pandemics more successfully.

As we settle into more comfortable years, we should never forget that there is an invisible destroyer looming beyond every magnificent sunrise.

But there is something even more important for us to remember.

As the stories presented in this book demonstrate, an imperceptible enemy can damage and kill many among us, but it cannot destroy the human spirit. Even without immunity, we have something powerful within us that always claims victory.

With each calamity, selfless heroes ascend: People who are willing to sacrifice their personal comfort and well-being for the comfort and well-being of others. People who refuse to cower in the face of danger. People who recognize that a life governed by panic and fear is no life at all. All of their stories stand as beacons of light for successive generations to learn from, find strength in, and build upon.

It is our responsibility to ensure that the individual stories captured and preserved today are retold and carved into the expanding granite walkway of the human narrative.

Made in the USA
Columbia, SC
16 April 2020